• • •

Unposted Letter is life's wisdom unfolded in simple, but in most effective manner. We begin our daily Senior Management meeting by listening to one 'wisdom' from Unposted Letter and it has brought significant changes in the way we look at life.

Murugavel Janakiraman
CEO Matrimony.com

I usually read one article at random every night. Short, powerful insights, that amazingly gives the clarity I need at that point of time. It is like a Google that answers any question I have in my mind at that moment, only the answers are from my beloved Mahatria.

G. R. 'Anand' Ananthapadmanabhan
GRT Group

If there is one source that is influencing my thoughts and the being that makes a difference in this world through my work, it is Mahatria. This book will become THE starting point and a catalyst for anyone's awesome journey ahead. Everyone deserves it. Begin your journey today.

Atul N. Shah, *MD, FACAAI, FAAAAI,*
Medical Director, Center for Asthma & Allergy, NY, USA

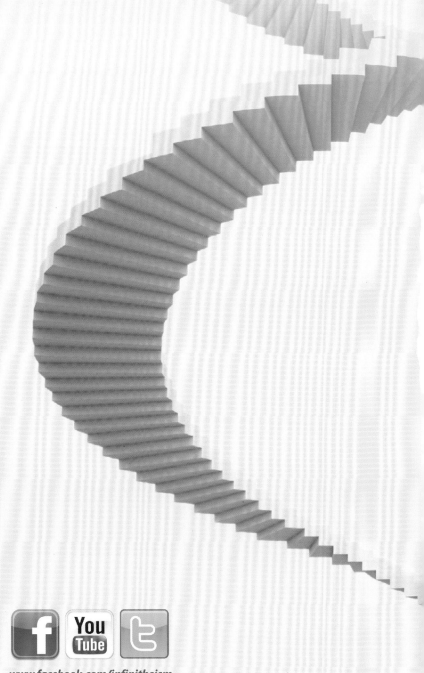

www.facebook.com/infinitheism
www.youtube.com/infinitheism
www.twitter.com/mahatria
www.infinitheism.com

•••

infinitheism

is the path that provides breakthroughs
for anyone who ardently desires **Most and more...**
in any sphere of human endeavour -
spiritual, emotional and material -
by transforming the human spirit to have faith
in its humongous, infinite potential.

To stephanie

From: Hetal

'14.

Carry me with you in life,
and I will carry you through life.

Published by **FROZEN THOUGHTS**
3, 3rd Cross Road, R A Puram,
Chennai, Tamil Nadu, India.
books@frozenthoughts.com
www.frozenthoughts.com

Printed at Srinivas Fine Arts (P) Ltd,
Keelathiruthangal, Sivakasi, Tamil Nadu

©2009

Unposted Letter
Self-Help
ISBN 978-81-9038-160-4

First Print: 2009
First to Fifth Print till November 2011 - 1,00,000 copies
Sixth Print - May 2013 - 25,000 copies

●●●

My Dear Readers,

**Open any page.
An answer is seeking the seeker.**

I dedicate this book to you.
It is your questions that the answers
unfolded through me. In that sense, you are
the co-author of this book.

Within its pages you will find solutions
that will enable you to realise the humongous,
boundless potential of the human spirit.
This book is for you, who desire abundance
in any of your endeavours -
spiritual, emotional and material.
You will find significant breakthroughs
to live a life of Most and more...

mahātria Rā

Unposted Letter

Table of Contents

Table of Contents

Table of Contents

●●●

My dear readers,

My life has taught me life. Every seeker who came to me for transformation in some way transformed me. My every student has been my teacher. I want to freeze my understanding and comprehension of life. Books are basically thoughts frozen in print. Hence this piece you are holding in your hands, 'Unposted Letter', through which, I want to enter your mind and your heart. Please, let me in...

Einstein invested his entire life and gave some theories to the world and the world has not been the same ever since. Edison's life changed the lifestyle of the rest of the world. Mahatma Gandhi and Nelson Mandela gave birth to a new culture. Milton and Tagore redefined poetry. Thyagaiya redefined music. Zakir Hussain brought a new status to the tabla. Roger Bannister and Edmund Hillary redefined human abilities. Socrates, Aristotle and Plato changed the thinking of the world. Every human life not only has the power to lift itself, but also has the power to lift the collective consciousness of humanity.

Many of our predecessors have already played their part in the evolution of human consciousness, and we are enjoying the benefit of it. What part are we going to play?

This is my humble attempt in that direction... to make a difference to my dear readers.

Mahatria Rā.

● ● ●

'Today' is His gift unto you.

Recognising the heart behind the material makes it a gift. Even a gift is just a material if you don't see the heart behind the material.

A pen becomes a gift when you recognise the heart that gave you that pen. You say, "I had a gifted childhood," when you recognise the heart of your parents in your upbringing. Education becomes a gift when you recognise the heart of the teachers who transferred that knowledge unto you. Lifestyle becomes a gift when you recognise the heart of your employers in your growth. Organisational growth becomes a gift when you recognise the heart of your employees in their endeavour.

A gift is not a material, but an outlook - to look out at the heart behind the material.

In that sense, 'Today' is an eternal gift. While there can be several sources for every gift, 'Today' is that precious gift that you either get from Him, or it just means that you have already lived your last day. Not everyone who went to sleep last night woke up this morning. The very fact you did, some force above still thinks you are worthy of another 'Today'. Recognise the heart of the divine behind this 24-hour material. Know, 'Today' is a providential gift. Realise, abusing the gift is abusing the giver. Wasting a day of your life will amount to abusing the giver of this gift. Only when you know the value of a gift, you will value the gift. Value 'Today' and make it valuable.

Today you will trade one day of your life for what you will get in return. So, make your today as productive as you can. Today is the first day of the rest of your life. So, draw a line to your past, believe yesterday was over yesterday, and press your speed button into your future. Today does not care about the blemishes of your past, nor is it affected by the uncertainties of the future - it is a day in itself, an opportunity in itself, and a portion of life by itself. So, take care of your Today(s) and you will take care of your life.

Buddha said, "Let us rise up and be thankful, for if we didn't learn a lot today, at least we learned a little, and if we didn't learn a little, at least we didn't get sick, and if we got sick, at least we didn't die; so, let us all be thankful."

Pray, "Oh my lord, this day of mine is your gift unto me and the way I live this day will be my gift unto you."

• • •

There is no easy way to the top.

W hen you choose to drive, you have to accept traffic jams. When you choose to be health conscious, you have to forego being tongue conscious. With income will come income tax.

Anything you choose in life comes along with its own inherent positives and negatives. What folly it is to search for a rose bush without the thorns! When you choose one face of the coin, you have also chosen the other side of the coin. Don't ask for a trouble-free, blessed life. Not even the mahatmas could embrace a trouble-free blessed life. There is no such life.

Bigger the ambition, greater will be the issues. When you want to walk, the issues are few. When you choose to run a marathon, obviously there are more issues to deal with. When you choose to merely exist, you face lesser issues. When you choose to live worthy of your potential, then you have to solve larger issues. By lifting one end of the stick, you have already picked up the other end. Only if you are willing to be chiselled, you will become the idol worthy of being worshipped. There is no easy way to the top, and those who made it to the top didn't make it easy.

After all, there has to be a difference between a history reader and a history maker.

In a Bible study group, they read Malachi 3:3: "He will sit as a refiner and purifier of silver." What did it mean about the character and nature of God? That week, one of the women had an appointment with a silversmith to watch him at work. As she watched the silversmith, he held a piece of silver over the fire and let it heat up. He explained that one had to hold the silver in the middle of the fire where the flames were hottest for all the impurities to get burnt away. She asked the silversmith if it was true that he had to sit there in front of the fire the whole time. The man affirmed that he not only had to sit there holding the silver, but also had to keep his eyes on the silver the whole time. If the silver was left a moment too long in the flame, it would be destroyed. The woman then asked, "How do you know when the silver is fully refined?" He smiled and answered, "Oh, that's easy... when I see my image in it."

If you are feeling the heat of life, remember that God has His eye on you and will keep watching you until He sees His image in you. In every man sleeps a prophet. God became man, so that man can again become god. Life isn't a furnace that's burning you, but one that's transforming you into glittering silver.

•••

A relationship that matters to you the most...

If you are happy in life right now, it's not because everything about your life is necessarily going right, but because a relationship that really matters to you the most is going great. If you are unhappy in life right now, it's not because everything about your life is going wrong, but because a relationship that really matters to you the most is not going great.

Relationships are like seeds. They have to be nurtured and developed. Expectations are like weeds. They grow on their own accord. When enough investment goes into building a relationship, the expectations in that relationship can be managed. When a relationship is left neglected, then the expectations in that relationship shake the very roots of the relationship. Our problem is growing expectations in stagnant relationships.

Let us use the metaphor of a savings bank account. Deposits build the reserves in an account from which we can withdraw - but we can withdraw only to the extent we have built the reserves. Similarly, withdrawals in a relationship are possible only to the extent we have made deposits in that relationship.

In a relationship where there is substantial emotional reserve, mistakes will be tolerated and forgiven, the meaning will be understood even when communication is inadequate, and your intentions will be appreciated even if you fall short in your actions. In all, the relationship will be good because you are considered good. And you are considered good because of the deposits you have made to build the emotional reserves in that relationship.

However, there are some relationships which are taken for granted; the permanence of the relationship is assumed, and nothing is done to nurture the relationship. Expectations continue to rise, but the investments needed to build the relationship are not made with the same continuity. The emotional reserves are overdrawn. In such a scenario, you will be held an offender for every word you speak; every move of yours will be judged; verbal battles and slammed doors will become regular occurrences; neither will your actions be appreciated, nor will your intentions be respected. Such a relationship is like walking on a minefield - it blows up any time and many times.

The solution is simpler than simple. Deposits, more deposits and many more deposits. No active relationship can be free from withdrawal, but we can always make enough deposits. That on which you invest time grows. Relationships have to be nurtured with the investment of quality time. Take time to listen and to understand. As often as possible, communicate to be understood. Make your love visible by being expressive and demonstrative. Seek to give, but also be graceful in receiving. Receiving is one way of showing your respect for the giver, and it is a huge deposit. Deposit by deposit, build a great relationship and thus earn your happiness in life.

Mythology shows that even gods had problems in relationships. Here is an opportunity to be one up on god.

● ● ●

For our children,
we are the only Koran they
will read in their lifetime;
the only Vedas they will see;
the only Bible they will experience;
the only Dharma they will follow.

Your life and my life will either serve
as a Warning or as an Example.

I know it is an awesome responsibility,
but how else can you explain
why you came into this planet
before them?

You are more important than every THING that has come into your life.

The husband gifted a new car to his wife for her birthday. He first handed over the keys, then a pouch with all necessary documents, including her driving license, and followed it up with a long hug. He then offered to take care of the children and asked her to go on a long drive. She thanked him with a kiss and she was gone with her auto-baby. Hardly a kilometre into the drive, she hit a median. She was safe, but the car was dented. She was consumed with guilt, "What will I tell him? How will he take it?" Thoughts and feelings ran amok. The police were quick to arrive at the accident scene. "Can we see your license?" they demanded. Her hands still shivering, she reached for the pouch that her husband had given her.

With tears rolling down her cheeks, as she picked the license from the pouch she noticed a 'post it' on it with her husband's handwriting, "Honey, in case of an accident, please remember, it is you that I love and not the car. Loving you."

Blessed are those who have understood that they should be loving people and using things, and not loving things and using people.

A scratch on the car makes our blood pressure go up… but we don't seem to mind a scratch in our heart. I know of a man who broke an artefact by intentionally throwing it on the floor and then remarked, "For eighteen years it has been giving me tension - if it breaks, if it falls down… I thought it was time to show who the boss is and gain some peace of mind." I know of another person who gave a party because his Mercedes Benz was rammed and jammed in an accident. He explained, "Though the car is completely damaged, nothing happened to me, who was inside the car. Now that I am okay I can buy another car, but if the automobile was intact and I was gone - it wouldn't have made much sense."

Our life began with the 60-rupee toy car. When it broke, we cried. Then we upgraded ourselves to the 2000-rupee remote-controlled car. When that got damaged, we wept. Then we were gifted the 20,000 rupee battery-operated car. When that stopped working, we were depressed. Then came the 4-lakh car, after that the 22-lakh SUV, followed by the 86-lakh luxury sedan... And, every time something happened to this machine, whether a scratch or a dent, the mercury of our tensions and worries went up. All in all, it seems our toys have grown, but we haven't. What we cry for has changed, but the crying is still on. Just that our crying is a lot more sophisticated now. It has many new names like anger, disappointment, frustration, stress, anxiety, etc...

Toys are there to entertain us. Toys have only one purpose: to be useful to us. From your beach house to your SUV to your latest gizmos and everything else... everything exists to make your life more comfortable. You are bigger than every THING you own. You are more precious than every THING you possess. You are more important than every THING that has come into your life.

A toy is just a toy. Buy toys. Buy more and more toys. But give them their rightful place. They are just there to be useful to you, to make your life comfortable and to entertain you. Don't ever waste another drop of your precious tears for a toy, no matter how dear the toy may be. After all, you are the dearest of them all.

• • •

The fact is "We Don't"
and not "We Can't."

It does not matter
how much we have,
but what really matters is
what we do with what we have.

We cannot do much to change
what we have, but we can
certainly change the way we use
what we have.

A pawn, if used well,
will become the queen.

• • •

The vital few and the trivial many.

V ilfredo Pareto, the Italian economist, discovered the 80/20 principle in 1897, which is now referred to as Pareto's rule. He discovered that 80% of the output results from 20% of the input, 80% of consequences flow from 20% of causes, and 80% of results come from 20% of effort. Joseph Juran referred to this 20% as the 'vital few' and the 80% as the 'trivial many'. Sir Isaac Pitman, who invented shorthand, discovered that just 700 common words make up two-thirds of our conversation. He found that these words account for 80% of common speech.

A student covers 80% of his syllabus in 20% of his study hours. About 80% of the question paper in the examination is from 20% of the syllabus. About 20% of customers contribute to 80% of growth, profitability and satisfaction; 20% of products and services account for 80% of the turnover; 20% of employees generate 80% of productivity; the opinion of 20% defines the society; the output of 20% of the population defines the economy of a country.

If you have 20 sales people, four will be great, six will be mediocre, and ten will simply be hanging in there. Sales managers make the mistake of working with the under-producers and non-performers, trying to get them to be more productive, while the top performers go unattended and are taken for granted. The easiest way to lose your top sales producers is to ignore them in favour of the 'trivial many'. Focus on the strong and make them stronger.

80/20 thinking is the secret of achieving more with less. Start celebrating exceptional productivity instead of trying to raise the average effort. Strive for excellence in a few things rather than good-enough performance in many.

There is a tragic amount of waste everywhere. Almost four-fifth of everything that is happening in your life is yielding very little in return. Too much focus is on the 80% which yields only 20%. Transform your thinking. Revamp your outlook. Reallocate your resources from the unproductive 'trivial many' to the productive 'vital few'. Effectiveness is not about what happens to the 80%, but about how you manage, control and utilise the 20%. 20% of your time actually defines what you are and what you will be in life.

Focus on the 20% and 80% of everything in your life will be taken care of.

• • •

The need to be respected
is far greater than the
need to be guided.

Even before she could learn to possess, she was asked to share. When she was barely five, she was asked to make sacrifices for the sake of her brother who was just two. She was still a kid, but her parents expected her to play the role of a responsible older sister. Thirty years later, she has a family of her own; so does her brother. She still feels responsible for her younger brother. She still advices him... interferes whenever there are ripples in her brother's marriage, advices her brother's wife on what to feed the child, and how to parent the child. She is still making sacrifices, but what is she getting in return?

Heartaches, sleepless nights and copious tears over being treated with indifference. Why? Her brother is old enough to make his own decisions. Even if some of his decisions go wrong, he feels he has the right to make those mistakes; he feels they are his learning ground. The sister-in-law regards her as unwanted interference in her marriage. She believes she should have the freedom to parent her children the way she wants and detests the idea of others interfering under the guise of being older to her.

From the first word uttered to the first word written to the first steps he walked... the father played an active part in it. For the son, his dad was always a superman, a hero and the only role model he wanted to emulate. Even the son's career counselling was done by Dad. The son went on to become a first-generation entrepreneur and again it was his dad who guided him. Today, the son is a celebrated industrialist. Even today, the Dad waits up every evening to know what happened at work, but the son feels claustrophobic. He feels that his dad should give him more space. Dad is going through spells of depression because he's not getting the same attention he used to get from his son. Dad feels that he's not needed anymore. The effect of this is showing up on his health - he is beginning to age a little faster.

You can always be a sister, but you cannot always play the sister. You will always be loved as a parent, but you cannot always play the parent. Beyond a point, not everybody can accept a 'holier-than-thou' approach.

A three-year-old expects to be respected in a certain way and the three-year-old needs to be respected that way. At three, not being given the choice of clothes she wants to wear is interpreted by her as not being respected. At ten, the son wants to read the menu card by himself and place the order. That to him is his idea of being respected. As a teenager, she wants to choose her friends; and her parents respecting her choice of friends is her sense of being respected. Now that he has worked with you for a few years, he wants to take a few decisions by himself, and your not overruling his decisions is his sense of being respected. Every age and every phase of life has some sense of respect associated with it, and you need to respect that.

Though the intentions may be noble, sometimes our attempt to guide people, especially unasked for, makes them feel not respected. The need to be respected is far greater than the need to be guided.

Make others feel respected... let this be your choice. They will take your guidance... let this be their choice.

● ● ●

To live is to live fearlessly.

*When you have nothing to hide,
you have nothing to avoid.*

*True freedom is found
only in transparent living.*

*The greatest compliment
one can give oneself
is to declare,
"I am an open book."*

● ● ●

Life will not postpone
our death. So, let us
not postpone our life.

W hat causes management stress? It is caused by the gap between when a thing should have been done and when it was eventually done. What is Technology gap? It is a better way of doing things that has already come into the industry, but you are yet to implement.

If what has to be done has to anyhow be done eventually, then why not do it today and save the stress? If there is a better way of doing things, then why not get to it before someone else does and enjoy that edge... rather than being an also-ran? When we know that something is bad, then why not drop it now? Why wait for the New Year? Why wait for another day?

Do you want to deliver 'world-class' quality? From this very moment, stop doing anything that is less than 'world-class' quality. Do you want to apologise for a mistake you committed earlier but have just become aware of... seek forgiveness immediately; else, you'll reel with guilt. Had a flash of brilliance... execute the idea immediately, else someone else will and you will merely follow.

Fools and wise men do the same things, but at different times. Wise men do it at once and fools do it at last. Live as if tomorrow is today.

We understand the importance of health and fitness, but postpone our efforts in that direction. We realise the importance of financial planning and investment, but procrastinate taking the initiative in that direction. We comprehend the importance of our board exams, but push our preparations till it becomes a crisis. We find pushing papers into the pending folder the most convenient option.

All stress and tension in life is nothing but the accrual of psychological pressure caused by the gap between when something should have been done and when it was eventually done. Procrastination is the most certain way to shorten one's lifespan. Postponement is the signature of underachievers.

Life will not postpone our death. So, let us not postpone our life.

There is no such day as 'one of these days'. Today is the day. If tomorrow comes, I will tell tomorrow, 'I've already done it yesterday'.

Where man's responsibility ends, Existential responsibility takes over.

There is a subtle difference between 'waiting' and 'waiting for', and in that lies the difference between 'peaceful progress' and 'stressful success'.

The farmer has ploughed the soil and planted the seeds... now he must wait... Where man's responsibility ends, existential responsibility takes over. Now if the farmer knows the art of 'waiting', he will wait peacefully. Instead, if he waits for the sprouting, then every passing moment will make him restless and stressed. His mind will keep rattling - "Why isn't it happening? Why not yet?" Even if it eventually sprouts, he has already traded his peace for success. The damage is already done.

Have you pressed the button for the elevator... now wait... it will come when it comes. 'Waiting for' the

---

elevator will make you pace the floor and make your eyeballs go up and down... as if that will speed up the elevator and make it reach your floor faster. Have you placed your order with the waiter... just wait... waiting for the waiter will make the wait an exasperating experience. Have you taken the decisions that are to be taken... have you performed the actions that are to be performed... have you done what can be done by you... now wait... just wait... not 'for' this or that or anything, but just wait... In it, you will discover the key to peaceful progress. 'Waiting for' also brings in success, but that success is far too stressful. When there is a peaceful path to success, why take the stressful path?

One of the most essential qualities for spiritual progress is the ability to do one's part and just wait... Most people who cry for a spiritual experience, that eluding silence, actually suffer because of this attitudinal disease - waiting for. By 'waiting for' the experience, you become a witness against your own self, instead of becoming a witness to the experience. It is to that 'waiting witness' that the spiritual experience unfolds itself.

Give up 'waiting for' and you will give up stressful success. Learn to do your part and wait... that's the path to peaceful progress.

●●●

Life has sent a teacher, disguised as experience.

Our maturity is always one leg below every new experience we encounter in life. The very purpose of life's experiences is to give us that maturity... but then, with every experience it isn't just the bar of our maturity that gets raised a little, even the bar of challenges we face gets raised. Thus goes the upward growth spiral of life.

It is immaterial how knowledgeable we are, or how much of life we have seen, or if we are the very best in what we do - even if we are an encyclopaedia on life... a fall, a trip, a slump is always round the corner. Life always intrudes to disturb the flow, the rhythm...

But remember, on the totem pole of growth, a failure in the tenth grade is still higher than a pass in the eighth grade. A just-miss in an attempt to scale Mount Everest is still a leg higher than making it to the top of the local hill. The higher the maturity, the higher the challenge. That's how life moulds man.

Life isn't a journey of going two steps forward and one step back. That happens only when man lives his life without awareness... without learning from his experiences. A man whose awareness coaches him to learn from every experience lives as though he's on a trampoline - he rises to fall and falls to rise... but the rise after every fall is even higher. Both his maturity and the level of his challenges are raised to the next higher leg.

What is the reason for your success? "Good decisions." What enables you to make good decisions? "Life's experiences." How do you gain life's experiences? "Bad decisions."

On the trampoline of life's experiences, I keep growing experience by experience. Every experience either gives me what I want, or it gives me the awareness - why I didn't get what I want.

The next time a setback disturbs your centeredness... just remember, life has sent a teacher, disguised as experience, to help you raise the bar of your maturity. Let your awareness help you to not only mature out of that experience, but also regain your centeredness. Get ready for a higher challenge. We mortals have to fall to rise... the blessing being that we always rise a little higher.

•••

Much after 'your' life and 'my' life has become 'our' life...

Existence has purposefully created man and woman a little incomplete so that they could embrace each other and make it complete. However, centuries of conditioning have given the terms husband and wife a very narrow connotation. It has shrunk the scope of this relationship. Drop the words husband and wife from your vocabulary and resolve to be 'friends for a lifetime'. Then, both the man and the woman will sometimes play the mother, sometimes the father, sometimes a cranky kid, then the mentor, the teacher, the mirror... and of course, sometimes husband and wife too. Expand the definition of this relationship and keep it open.

Dignity in a marital relationship is found when you relate to your spouse as a complete individual, and not just the body. Observe each other's way of thinking, discuss personal values, standpoints and convictions; get sensitised to each other's feelings, develop emotional compatibility and take time to sit together in quietude to develop spiritual connectivity. Respect the entirety of the person and relate to the whole person, not just the peripheral aspect of the other - the body.

Don't try to do in one year what can be done in ten years and don't try to do in one month what can be done in one year. Most married couples fall all over each other, overdo everything within the first few months and then there is no life left in that relationship. They coexist in a dead relationship. What can be a tree should not die as a plant. Take it slow and make it long.

In life, as well as in a good relationship, the past is irrelevant. The present forms the building blocks. The future is very significant, for that is where the two of you will travel together. Discussing day-to-day trifles alone will only make you fall in love. Talk future, talk dreams, talk ambitions, and resolve to play a part in each other's growth in a very objective and nonintrusive manner. That's the way to grow in love.

There is this universal concept that after the wedding, both lives superimpose and there is only one life to live from then on. As a result, women were often forced to live as a shadow of their man in the name of marriage. They tagged on, but as frustrated, selfpitying, sacrificial individuals who felt exploited. The fact is, much after YOUR life and MY life has become OUR life, there is still my life and your life. 'Our' life is that intersecting space called marriage. Happiness in marriage depends on how both relate in 'our' space and how this space keeps growing with every passing year. However, he will continue to have his life and she should continue to have her life. In fact, she is at her best in 'our' space when she goes to her space and then comes to 'our' space; the same is true with him. This will ensure that you respect each other's space, each other's individual likes, dislikes and priorities, and most importantly, this alone will ensure that you do not suffocate each other in the name of love.

Marriage, in its true sense, should improve the quality of life of both involved. Marriage can and should be a continuity of life, magnifying the possibilities for both.

A good marriage has to be nurtured and developed. Building a great marriage is an art; so get artistic.

• • •

*It is not the question of whose
mistake it is in a relationship;
it is a question of whose life!*

*Instead of accepting
yourself as you are and
expecting the world to change
accept the world as it is and
you start changing your approach
towards the world.*

*Let life be beautiful
because of the world.*

*Let life be beautiful
in spite of the world.*

●●●

Which of your customers are you planning to fire?

Even if an organisation is progressing exceptionally well, not all their staff will be competent and committed people, there will be some average ones and of course, a few troublemakers too... They come as an integrated package. Ironically, the energy, time and effort that gets sapped in managing the few troublemakers is no less compared to leading the competent and committed majority. Why give the few so much of you? Why not fire them and invest the resource saved on the productive ones?

One rotten tomato will soon spoil all the other tomatoes. Haven't you noticed a non-performer soon forms a team of other non-performers around him? If you can't mend them, end them. Throw the rotten tomato out and save the good tomatoes. Do I sound apathetic? Any organisation that sympathises with non-performers will soon need the sympathy of others.

There's nothing revolutionary about this idea... many organisations are already practicing it.

Now my question is, "Why not sack a few of your existing clients?" Isn't it true that the energy, time and effort that gets sapped in managing the few troublemaking clients is no less compared to servicing many of your genuine, loyal, major accounts? There are some who will remain dissatisfied, no matter what you do. No matter how you serve them, they will keep criticising your product and service. There are also those who believe in making you go down on your knees for every payment. Finally when the payment is made, you make no profit out of such deals... the interest you paid for the delay would have already eaten into your margins. Why not fire some of those clients from your client list and invest the resource saved on some of your major accounts?

The customer is always right - right? Wrong! The customer is the king - isn't he? Not always... it depends on who the customer is.

The search is not merely for customers, but for good customers. And, it is for good customers alone, you become their solution-provider, and they become a partner in your growth. Truly, a win-win situation.

So, which of your customers are you planning to fire with immediate effect? Oh, that's a revolutionary idea.

• • •

Get ahead of people.
Do not get
even with them.

My friend and I recently visited a home for abandoned children. There we spoke to a staff member, who was very affable by nature, about wanting to make a material contribution to the home. He told us that we would have to discuss that with one of their social workers who was in charge of receiving contributions. While we were waiting, a lady walked in. In a tone so arrogant that it would have made Adolph Hitler turn in his grave, she said, "Oh, you people want to make a contribution! Give me 500 kilograms of rice... I only want that now. I am not interested in taking anything else. Of course, if you people can't afford it, then give me 5 kilograms of rice... but I want rice and nothing else. I am leaving." No courtesy, no pleasantness, no smile... She just walked in, did some verbal vomiting and walked out. "She is in charge of receiving contributions!? God save the children of the home," I thought to myself.

My friend and I did not speak for quite some time... we were still reeling from that experience of utter disrespect and disregard. Later I told my friend, "Let's give them the 500 kilograms of rice. We want to make a difference to the children, not to the lady. Let her behaviour not stand as a wall between our hearts and the children's stomachs."

When you are recovering from an illness, doctors say, "You are responding to the medicine." If your health deteriorates, doctors say, "The medicine is reacting on you." Response is positive; reaction is negative. Let us never react to any situation in life, but instead choose our response. Let our behaviour not be instigated by forces from outside, but be born out of an internal value-based choice. Let not some man or woman in the world outside parade over our inherent goodness.

How the world behaves is none of our business. The greatest pride is in rising in your own eyes. How much ever you are tested, wherever you go, whatever you do... live your character.

Let the limitations of other people not limit us. 'Someone is wrong' isn't an excuse for us to be wrong. Wrong as a response to wrong isn't the way. Let us not trade our goodness. At every opportunity, let us get ahead of people and not get even with them.

● ● ●

Emotions - yes.
Emotional drama - no!

The husband and wife gifted themselves a new car for their first wedding anniversary. They drove downtown, zipped through the beach road, watched a movie in a drive-in theatre, and finally returned home. As they didn't have a garage, they parked the car on the street. When they woke up the next morning, they found to their utter shock that the car was missing. It had been stolen. Their first car, their first wedding anniversary gift, and they had barely enjoyed the car for a day. The wife couldn't take it. Misty-eyed, she sank into the sofa. The husband too was jolted, but his love for his wife prevailed over the moment. He hugged her from behind and said, "The car is lost. You can feel upset about it. The car is lost. You can take it easy. Either way, the car is lost. Then, why not take it easy?" She glared at him and the moment passed. Two months later, the police recovered the car from a car robbing gang, and the car was returned to the husband. That very evening, while driving back home from the police station, the husband rammed the car against a truck. This time it was his turn. He couldn't take it. On returning home, misty-eyed, he sank into the sofa. The wife too was jolted. But, her love for him prevailed over the moment. This time, she hugged him from behind, and said, "The car is rammed. You can feel upset about it. The car is rammed. You can take it easy. Either way, the car is rammed. Then, why not take it easy."

A logical question: When the car is lost or rammed, how can anyone take it easy? But what else can you do? Feel upset, if you want; take it easy, if you want - either way, after the emotional drama, what has to be done has to be done. The police complaint has to be lodged, the car has to be sent to the workshop, the insurance has to be claimed... what has to be done has to be done.

The child has failed in one of the subjects. The father slaps the child a few times. The mother hits herself on her forehead several times and cries. After all the emotional drama, what? Now, you will have to take greater care while coaching your child in that subject - he might perhaps require special tuition - what has to be done has to be done. You left the milk a little longer than required on the gas stove. The boiled milk is beginning to overflow from all sides of the vessel. Scream, wail, shout, get tense, and let your BP shoot up... after all the emotional drama, now what? You will switch the stove off, remove the vessel and clean the kitchen counter. Eventually, what has to be done will be done.

From a stock market crash to a key employee's resignation to the death of a loved one... after the emotional drama, eventually what has to be done will be done. Here we are not discussing about not being emotional, but about avoiding dramatic emotional reactions. Understandably, you will skip a heartbeat when you lose your vehicle, you will sink into helplessness when the child fails, legitimate tears will roll down at the loss of a beloved. Emotions - yes. Emotional drama - no!

Emotional Maturity is not about avoiding emotions, but it is about avoiding the emotional drama. Anyways, what has to be done has to be done. Then, why the drama?

• • •

How long will you bang against a wall?
You may begin to bleed, but the wall will
never open up for you.

How long will you curse your luck
and wait under a mango tree
expecting oranges?
You may drop dead,
but not a single orange
will drop from a mango tree.

What is, is.
What is not, is not.

Genius is in knowing
what to hold on and when to let go.

• • •

Let the good make noise.

An aspiring youth joined a daily as an apprentice. After three days of rigorous training and induction, he was asked to go to the field and come back with a story worth publishing. After toiling through the streets and braving the heat for close to six hours, he was returning to office with a sense of failure as he hadn't collected a worthwhile story. He came to a junction where three roads met in a 'Y' formation. He noticed two buses speeding towards the junction from the two opposite roads, oblivious of what they were heading for. An accident seemed almost inevitable. The young reporter used his presence of mind, ran to the meeting point of the two roads, vigorously waved both his hands, screamed at the top of his voice and eventually succeeded in stopping both the buses. Hundreds of passengers from both the buses took the youth's hand into theirs and thanked him... some even kissed him. However, on hearing this heroic story from the young reporter, the editor of the newspaper sacked him saying, "You missed a golden opportunity of a dramatic story worthy of headlines."

We do not live in a bad world. It's just that the bad makes news. In a world where the bad makes so much noise, we need more and more avenues through which the good too will begin to make noise. We cannot remain taciturn anymore. Smoking, drinking, chewing and many other harmful habits are advertised enough; but what is available to brainwash the world on all the good activities?

Tax evaders make headlines… instead, why not a story on the front page about the taxpayers? The photos of murderers are flashed… instead, why not that of lifesavers? Why not a story about a soldier every day?

Go out into the world and speak all the good you know of all the people. Tell your friends about the virtues of your parents. Let everyone in your club know how proud you are of your children. Stick a bulletin about all the qualities you admire in your teachers. Gossip more and more about all the extraordinary things ordinary people around you are doing every day of their lives. Write to your in-laws about how blessed you are to have their child as your spouse. Shout, scream, write, speak, blow the trumpet, make noise… make noise… about all the good that you can see.

Let us together impress the world and impress upon the world that our world is actually a good world…

●●●

*Any attraction needs
a distraction.
Without breaks,
we will break down.*

Resting Heart Rate (RHR) is the rate at which your heart beats when you wake up in the morning, but when you are still in bed. A low RHR indicates that the heart is resting sufficiently between two successive contractions and expansions. A high RHR indicates that the heart does not rest enough between two successive contractions and expansions. So, lower the RHR, the healthier your heart is. The conclusion is that even the heart we sing praises of, for working from womb to tomb, takes enough rest for it to go on and on and on...

We have a very unfortunate misconception that holidays are only for the rich and the elite, and only for children who haven't yet begun to shoulder the responsibilities of life. We still consider going on holidays an expense. To most people, holidays are nothing more than religious holy days - a declared off from the workplace.

When the body or mind reaches its threshold, efficiency declines. As much as we take rest at the end of the day to replenish our energy levels, holidays rejuvenate our mind, intellect and emotions and thereby the spirit.

If at all we do go on a holiday, we exhaust ourselves with seeing seven different places in a day's time. It is plenty of travelling, sightseeing, visiting places of worship and endless shopping. Such holidays, instead of serving as a break, actually break you down. What to say of people who do the same even during their honeymoon!

Taking family holidays is the best investment one can make to rebuild family ties. Likewise, taking a holiday as an organisation greatly strengthens interpersonal relationships. It provides uninterrupted time with each other and hence reduces the accumulated emotional baggage. It breaks the pattern of routine life which has turned out to be a professional drill for most people. It not only provides recreation, but also re-creates your spirits (the solid one, not the liquid).

Leave your mobile phones, laptops and your tight inner garments behind. Dress comfortably during your holiday and forget modelling. Resolve not to call your office till your holiday is through. For heaven's sake, do not go there and start cooking your own food. Treat your toungue to new cuisines. You will come back feeling on 'Top of the World'. You will also realise that the 'World was not on your top' and it went on without you.

A holiday to unwind... a holiday to break the pattern of thought and work... a holiday to rejuvenate... a holiday to breathe different air... a holiday to look back and to look ahead... a holiday to dedicate yourself completely to the family... a holiday to be a full-time spouse, a full-time parent, and a full-time son... a holiday to free yourself from your labels and designations.

Any attraction needs a distraction. Holidays are mandatory. Without breaks, we will break down. Do you know that even God took a day off? "For in six days the Lord made heaven and earth, and on the seventh day He rested, and was refreshed." - Exodus 31:17.

• • •

Distractions are a must for Attraction.

*Every time you shift
from Activity-A to Activity-B
and then return to Activity-A,
the efficiency improves.*

*Monotony in any form must be broken.
Change in any form relaxes your mind.
And a relaxed mind always thinks better.*

*That's why people always think well
in the lap of nature, as nature provides
all the creative distractions that are
needed to deepen one's attraction.*

• • •

It is not right and wrong.
It is about compatibility.

Y ou desire a 20' x 16' room and your architect thinks a 16' x 16' room is enough. One idea is not better than the other, but it is 'what you want' versus 'what you get'. As an architect, it is 'what you want to give' versus 'what your client wants to take'. It is not about right and wrong, good and bad, better and best; but it's all about compatibility and synergy.

A square is as good as a circle. So, when there is a square peg in a square hole and a round peg in a round hole, there are no issues. The issue is only when we try to fit a square peg in a round hole. What a toothpick can do, a bulldozer cannot. Sometimes the best is not good enough. A sunflower is beautiful, but in a rose garden, it will be treated as a weed.

Bring a man who has worked in a system-driven organisation into a developing organisation, and he will create a huge imbalance. Again, someone who is used to power, position and protocol can never feel comfortable in a flat organisational structure. Such people cause a lot of resignations and eventually they too will quit. There is no questioning the capability of these people; it's just that a round peg won't fit in a square hole.

We look for qualifications, experience, brilliance, skills and attitudes, performance background, age, sex, etc., when we should actually be asking this question - "Is he compatible with the prevailing culture of my organisation?"

We look for looks, family and educational background, religion, community, when we should actually be asking this question, "Will she be compatible with our family?" So what if he is working in an MNC, so what if he is highly educated, so what if he is 6' 2", he wants a homemaker and you are highly career-oriented. All other factors fail on this one incompatibility. You are a connoisseur of good food and you get married to a woman who extends a Pizza Hut menu card every time you speak of dinner.

Individual brilliance is very different from collective brilliance. True, the knight is more powerful than the pawn, but when you are playing the white pieces, isn't the white pawn a greater asset to you than the black knight?

With compatibility, 1 + 1 is 3. Without it, 1 + 1 is 0.

• • •

Nothing like growing in the right hands.

How often we meet people who keep cursing their fate for having studied with the regional language as their medium of instruction? With a year's formal training, they can learn the language they want to and knock that weakness off. How often people suffer the inconvenience of the driver not turning up for work! Immobile, despite the fact that an automobile is staring at them from their own garage. With a month's formal training, they can learn driving and knock a weakness off. Fear of public speaking is rated next only to the fear of death. Yet, through formal training, one can master public speaking in a matter of weeks.

When a weakness, a limitation, can be knocked off, why suffer it and let it incapacitate us for the rest of our lives? Invest some time in training, knock a weakness off and enjoy its benefit for the rest of your life!

Formal, systematic training not only enables us to overcome our limitations, but also helps us to become better at what we are already good at.

Anyone can run. However, if you want to be an athlete, you have to undergo formal, systematic training. Scribbling becomes writing under formal, systematic training. Talking becomes communication under formal, systematic training. Exercise under formal, systematic training becomes a wellness program. If you want to play the game of chess, learn it from anybody; but, if you want to become a champion, then you'll need systematic coaching from a trained coach. Yoga and meditation, if it is not meant to be a mere pastime, undergo formal initiation.

Nothing like our grandmother's remedies, yet don't we rush her to a doctor when she is sick? There is no substitute for formal, systematic training. Often, the difference between good, better and the best lies in the quality of training.

Muhammad Ali once said, "I hated every minute of training, but I said, Don't quit. Suffer now and live the rest of your life as a champion."

Ability, when subjected to systematic training becomes proficiency. There is no other way to be the best. Nothing like growing in the right hands.

• • •

What must be faced,
must be faced,
sooner rather than later.

"When was the last time you got your Master health check-up done?" the doctor enquired. "No doc, I have never got a Master health check-up done," the man replied. "Why so?" queried the surprised doctor, and added, "Post 40, you should get a Master health check-up done every two years." The man said, "I don't want to doc. Then they will come up with reports that may say my cholesterol level is high or I am diabetic... god knows, what else. Now I am absolutely fine. One health check-up and I will start feeling like a sick man."

Knowing very well escapism can only be transitory, and also knowing very well that you cannot eternally escape anything in life, why do you still try to escape?

Why do you hope against hope? Why is that you don't want to know what you must know? Just because you close your eyes, it doesn't mean that the world will become blind. Eventually, what must be faced must be faced. Then, why at all eventually? Why at all postpone? Why at all delay? The forest fire you will face tomorrow is the little spark that you tried to escape yesterday.

It is a fact that most of us lack the courage to face the facts of life. That we lack the courage to face the facts of life is the first brutal fact that we must face.

I think my friend is drifting away from me. Only if you face this fact, something can be done about it. I think his friends are influencing our son more than we are able to as parents. A hard fact, no doubt, but only in facing it can something be done about it. I think my marriage is falling apart. True, a heartbreaking fact, but the unwillingness to face this fact is not going to solve anything. I think the competition is eating into our market share. I think some of our employees are nurturing the aspirations of joining the competitor. I think my kind of work wins me not only friends, but also enemies. Though I have always told him that it was his mistake, I know in my heart of hearts that I was wrong. The list is endless...

Only if you face the fact, something can be done about it. If you avoid the fact, it gets nastier, and it revisits you. At least now, face the fact. Something can still be done about it. What you avoid does not go away from you. It gets uglier, and it revisits you. Every fact that you escape from will haunt you in the future with thoughts such as, "I should have... I could have... I must have..."

You can always seek the right medical intervention, follow the proper fitness regime and eat the right diet. You can ease out the differences with your friend through open communication; you can take the initiative to become your son's best friend, open up new markets, find a human beacon who can take you from here to there, and take the courage to say the small-big word 'Sorry'. Something can always be done. Face the brutal facts of life courageously; knowing very well, only then something can be done about it.

Everything that was ever solved was solved because somebody was willing to face it. It all starts with the courage to face the facts. In facing the facts that you had always tried to avoid, for the first time you are looking at life square in the eye. Escapism is not for people like you and me. What must be faced, must be faced, sooner rather than later.

●●●

Life is like a game of chess
and you play this game with Him.

After every move of yours,
He makes the next move.
Your moves are called 'Choices'
and His moves are called 'Consequences'.

You will be tested…
you will be challenged…
you will be pushed to the brink.

However, when you are found
to play your game well,
He wins by allowing you
to win the game.

• • •

Be someone's greatest gift.

I need a relationship in which I don't have to keep explaining myself. Nothing is more tiring than having to constantly explain yourself. Emotional tiredness drains you far more than physical tiredness. So, the search is for that one relationship in which I can enjoy the freedom of trust, where I don't have to explain everything about me.

I need a relationship in which I won't be held against myself. I have my strengths. I have my shortcomings. The search is for that one relationship in which my lesser side will not be provoked and instigated constantly. I want that one relationship in which my positives will always be brought to the surface.

I need a relationship in which my today is not viewed with the mistakes I made yesterday. Being human... I'm bound to err every now and then. I want someone who won't maintain a database of my mistakes. The search is for that relationship where yesterday's fight doesn't halt today's communication... where yesterday was over yesterday.

I need a relationship in which it isn't me who has to take the initiative all the time. I need a relationship where I can be transparent. I need a relationship in which I don't have to alter my likes and dislikes to gain and retain the relationship. I need a relationship in which my self-image is not scratched. I need a relationship in which I'm not asked to be anyone else. I need a relationship in which I feel completely myself... even more than when I am with my own self.

I need that one relationship in which I feel as though I am once again in my mother's womb... a relationship in which my heart always feels... just born.

Oh my dear readers, if you already have one such relationship... please go down on your knees in gratitude, for there cannot be a greater gift from life. Such a relationship is life's greatest gift.

If you don't have one, despair not. Didn't he say from the mountain top - "Do unto others what you want others do unto you"? Can you be that one to someone else? Gift ourselves into someone's life. Love someone so completely that you make yourself worthy of being someone's greatest gift.

People feel your love not by what you are with them, but by what they can be with you. In the presence and fragrance of your love, let your beloved blossom.

● ● ●

Your most precious
resource is yourself.
Are you using
yourself enough?

Japan decided to venture into manufacturing steel in the early 1960s. The two fundamental raw materials required for manufacturing steel are iron ore and coal, neither of which was available in Japan. But Japan knew where it could import these raw materials from - where they were available in abundance; and it also knew where to export its finished steel - where the demand was great. The result - by the late 1960s, Japan became the largest exporter of steel in the world. In less than a decade, an industrial revolution happened. How? Better resource management.

Let's say it costs 10 rupees to produce a product and it is sold at 11 rupees, with a profit margin of 1 rupee. One way of earning an additional rupee of profit is to generate another sale of 11 rupees, which means sales have to be increased by 100%. Another way is to find out how the product can be produced at 9 rupees, which means that the additional profit of one rupee can be earned with 10% improved production efficiency and the same amount of sales. No, I am certainly not advocating cutting corners or compromising on quality, but screaming 'better resource management'.

In most start-ups and medium-sized business units, the cost of their money - interest paid on borrowings - eats into their profits. When you audit their functioning, you realise that the problem isn't the lack of funds, but pathetic and inefficient fund management. Inefficiency in generation of cash flow and recklessness in managing cash outflow lead them into crisis-borrowing at higher rates of interest, thus eroding their profits. Year after year there is an increase in turnover, but inexplicably it doesn't translate as increase in profits. At the same time, observe well managed and efficiently led giants of organisations - every year they show growth in both turnover as well as profits. How? Better resource management.

Indians cry that population is their major problem. What has the world done about it? It has seen the same population as a source of efficient manpower at a lesser cost. The world has outsourced so much of their operations to India and improved their profitability. Better resource management. By luring multinationals to set up their operations in and around Dubai, Dubai has turned its barren deserts into an economic hub. Better resource management.

It's not that you don't have time; it's about managing the resource called time efficiently. It's not that you don't have enough space; it's about managing the resource called space efficiently. It's not that you don't have enough money, and hence you are not rich; it's about managing the resource called money, the little there is, efficiently enough to become rich.

Without iron ore and coal, Japan was able to become the largest exporter of steel in the 1960s. With nothing, Japan produced something. Then, we've got to believe that with something, everything can be achieved.

Somewhere in your life, some resource is either being wasted or being inefficiently managed. Find out what it is and improve upon it. Of course, your most precious resource is yourself. Are you using yourself enough?

• • •

There is no saturation in life...
only saturated minds.
There is no stagnation in life...
only stagnant people.

Life is a mere open parenthesis...
fill as much as you want...
there is no close parenthesis.

There is as much room
as your heart can conceive...
as much room
as your mind can believe...
as much room
as your attitude towards life.

The only word that can befit life is 'More.'

• • •

Either don't do it.
Or do it with devotion.
Nothing in between.

T ake a lemon and cut it into two. Use a squeezer and squeeze the juice into a glass. Add the required amount of sugar and a pinch of salt, preferably black salt. Fill the glass with cold water and stir thoroughly. The lime juice is ready. It's such a simple preparation and yet lime juice doesn't taste the same when made by two different people. Beyond lemon, sugar, salt and water, there is an invisible ingredient in the preparation of lime juice - and this invisible ingredient makes all the difference.

In everything we make, create and produce there is an invisible ingredient, and this invisible ingredient makes the difference between the better and the best, the ordinary and the extraordinary, the good and the excellent. Was the work done with love and happiness or was it performed with apathy and reluctance? The involvement of the heart in any task performed is that invisible ingredient. Is the heart 101% into what is being done - that's the crucial question.

I once told my daughter, "Kutti, either cook happily with love or don't cook at all. I can feel the difference in taste. Food that is served either has life or is just dead matter. The difference lies in how much heart went into making it."

Devotion is not a quality that should be reserved only for places of worship and altars of god. Devotion in everything we do... 101% of the heart's involvement in what we do is devotion. In dedication, you give of what you have and what you can. In devotion, you give yourself. Any work can become a prayer if performed with the sacredness of devotion.

The natural by-products of devotion are concentration, happiness and love. The precision, the finesse, the aura... devotion alone can achieve.

Tiredness and devotion are inversely proportional. Only when we begin to perform each and every act of ours with a sense of devotion will we realise one of the unspoken laws of nature, which is - 'Man was not designed for tiredness'. If you know a man who knows not tiredness, then know that you know a man for whom everything is an expression of devotion, and all his acts are acts of prayer.

Either don't do it. Or do it with devotion. Nothing in between.

• • •

*In prayer,
you talk to existence.
In meditation,
you listen to existence.*

*In prayer,
you listen to your own voice.
In meditation,
you listen to the beyond.*

*Prayer is
communication with existence.
Meditation is
a communion with existence.*

•••

Improve your capability.
Increase your capacity.
That's progress.

S top thinking, "This is the way we've always done it. So, this is the way it has to be done." Don't suffer from tradition paralysis. Nothing grows on ice. If we let our past freeze our minds, new ideas won't sprout. Stop backward, regressive thinking and start forward, progressive thinking. Absolute perfection in any human endeavour, from building satellites to rearing children, is unattainable. There is endless scope for improvement. Successful people know this. That's why they don't ask - "Can I do it better?" They know they can. So they ask the question, "How can I do it better?"

Man belongs to where he wants to go. Think 'improvement' in everything you do and think 'high standards' in everything you do. Believe it can be done. Believing something can be done sets the mind in motion to find a way of doing it. There is a way. And, there is a better way. When you believe it is impossible, your mind goes to work to prove why. But when you believe and really believe that something can be done, then your mind goes to work to help you find ways of doing it. Your mind will find a way, if you allow it to. Many of us whip and defeat our desires simply because we concentrate on why we can't, when the only thing worth concentrating on is why and how we can.

In almost everything in life, from work to home to community development, the formula for success is - 'do what you do even better' (improve the quality of your output) and 'do more of what you do' (increase the quantity of what you do). Qualitative upgradation plus quantitative growth is progress.

Constantly remind yourself that you are better than you think you are; so you can do everything in a better way than how you are already doing it. Also constantly remind yourself that you are not doing as much as you can; so you can do more of everything than what you are already doing.

Capability is the ability to better what you are already doing. Capacity is about doing more of what you are already doing.

Improve your capability. Increase your capacity. That's progress.

• • •

If only I had known that the end would be so beautiful...

He fractured his leg in an accident. It hampered his mobility and confined him to bed for several months. He was holding a good post in a leading MNC, which was now a thing of the past. An aged mother, who should be taken care of, was now taking care of him. Terrible days, hmm...? No, not all that terrible! This period gave the immobile soul unlimited time at his disposal. He made a brilliant choice - he gave all of it to reading. He nourished his inner being with some classic wisdom from thoughts of great people frozen in books. It was also the time when he developed a spiritual connectivity and realised that he should put his life on a purpose. Everything about his life changed... and it changed for ever. Today, he lives his purpose. Today his life is spiritually aligned. Today his life can be differentiated as - before the fracture and after the fracture. In one of the pages of his diary he wrote, "If only I had known that the end would be so beautiful, maybe I would have enjoyed it from the beginning."

I ask of you, "Would a loving parent ever give a child a story to read that doesn't have a happy ending?"

For all that the atma endured, we know him as the Mahatma. For all that she braved, the erstwhile schoolteacher was revered as Mother. In bearing the cross, he became a symbol of hope. Though born in prison, he lived as the lord of faith. It seems the end is always beautiful... There is always a bigger picture, way beyond our finite comprehension.

What is life without twists and turns? What is life without suspense and surprise? Call it tough times. Call it testing times. But a time will come when every man who asked, "Why me?" for his troubles, will ask, "Why me?" for his blessings.

The caterpillar wanted so much to become a butterfly that it went into a cocoon to grow wings. Sometimes life will throw you into a cocoon to help you to come out with flying colours. The bamboo was cut to become a flute. The stone was chiselled to become a statue. The gold was melted to become a jewel. You are tested only to be created. The story ahead is beautiful. You have to believe so. Your faith will be qualified, but then the return gift is a quality life.

You can go through anything in life, if you can eventually become what you can become.

• • •

Drop your labels.
You are enough...
...more than enough.

dvice her - "Why don't you take care of your
health," and your wife infers that as love. Tell
her, "As a husband, I think I have the right to
tell you to take care of your health," and she thinks you
are trying to dominate her. Ask him to have his lunch
on time and he will appreciate your concern. Instead
tell him, "I have seen my father too work, but he is not
like you. Why can't you eat on time?" You have to face
the longest face in town.

People cannot handle labels. People get ego involved
with labels. Labels close the minds of people.
Whatever is said under the guise of a label is never
received well.

Tell him, "Green leafy vegetables are good for you," and he will take it. Instead tell him, "As a strict vegetarian, I suggest that you start eating green leafy vegetables," and he will argue with you. The label 'vegetarian' is the problem.

Tell him, "Forgive her. Love even those who have hurt you," and he may heed to you. Tell him, "Being a true Christian, I request you to forgive and love even your enemies," and you are his next enemy. The label 'Christian' is the problem.

Tell her, "I wish our airports are more organised," and she will endorse your view. Tell her, "Having lived in Singapore, I know how organised things can be. I wish even our airports were more organised," and you will be considered a national outcast.

She has a problem with your Rotary involvement. One is anti-Brahmin and the other cannot trust people from Assam. 'All Marwaris are like that' is his foolish generalisation.

This is a human frailty. Man, when confronted with labels, somehow feels less about himself. So he tries to defend it with all his might. Inexplicably, labels make men suffer a complex. He has no problem with you. His problem is what you represent - the chair, the position, the religion, etc...

Why do we need labels? Is the position glorifying you or is it you who is glorifying the position? Does the chair need you or is it you who needs the chair? If labels alone define you, then you cannot do without the labels. Anyone who lives on the strength of labels can never have deep relationships. If you are the one who is adding value to the labels, then you don't need the labels. That's the beginning of deep relationships.

"Master, please accept me as your disciple," pleaded the seeker. "Tell me who you are," the Master asked. *"Ramachandra Rao."* "That's your name. Drop it and tell me who you are," the Master asked again. *"I am a businessman."* "That's your occupation. Drop it and tell me who you are." *"I am a man."* "That's your sex. Drop it and tell me who you are." *"Master, I no more know who I am!"* "That's good. That is the starting point for a seeker. When you drop all your labels and come as the pure you - that is the starting point for a seeker. Your business card works with the priest, but it has no value with god," the Master asserted.

Help yourself and help others by dropping your labels. You are enough... more than enough. Just the pure you - that is the starting point for everything. When you, as just you, are enough unto yourself - that's independence. In it is true freedom.

• • •

A bar of iron costs Rs.250...

made into a horseshoe,
its worth is Rs.1000;

made into needles,
its worth is Rs.10,000;

made into balance springs for watches,
its worth is Rs.1,00,000.

Your own value
is determined not by what you are,
but by what you are able to
make of yourself.

● ● ●

Money has no memory.
Experience has.

Y ou will never know the total cost of your education, but for a lifetime you will recall and relive the memories of school and college. A few years from now, you will forget the amount you paid for hospitalisation, but you will always cherish the memory of having saved your mother's life or the life you get to live with the newborn. You won't remember the cost of your honeymoon, but to the last breath remember the experiences of the bliss of togetherness. Money has no memory. Experience has.

Good times and bad times, times of prosperity and times of poverty, times when the future looked secure and times when you didn't know from where your tomorrow would come from… life has been in one way or another a roller-coaster ride for everyone. Beyond all that abundance and beyond all that deprivation, what remains is the memory of experiences. Sometimes the wallet was full... sometimes even the pocket was empty. There was enough and you still had reasons to frown. There wasn't enough and you still had reasons to smile. Today, you can look back with tears of gratitude for all the times you had laughed together, and also look back with a smile at all the times you cried alone. All in all, life filled you with experiences to create a history of your own self, and you alone can remember them all.

The first time you balanced yourself on your cycle without support...

The first time she said 'yes' and it was two years since you proposed...

The first cry... the first steps... the first word... the first kiss... all of your child...

The first gift you bought for your parents and the first gift your daughter gave you...

The first award... the first public appreciation... the first stage performance...

And the list is endless... Experiences, with timeless memory...

There's no denying that anything material costs money. But the fact remains that eventually the cost of the experience will be forgotten, but the experience never.

So what if there's an economic recession? Let it be, but let there not be a recession to the quality of your life. You can still take your parents, if not on a pilgrimage, at least to the local temple. You can still play with your children, if not on an international holiday, at least in the local park. It doesn't cost money to lie down or to take a loved one into your lap. Nice time to train the employees, create leadership availability and gear up for the wonderful time when they will arrive. And hey! Aspects like your health, knowledge development and spiritual growth are not economy dependent.

Time will pass... the economy will revive... currency will soon be current again... and in all this, I don't want you to look back and realise you did nothing but wallow in gloom. Recession can make you lose out on money. Let it not make you lose out on experiences... If you are not happy with what you have, no matter how much more you have, you will still not be happy.

Make a statement with the way you live your life: How I feel has nothing to do with how much I have.

• • •

At birth, your life was a plain canvas.
Your potential is the colours.
Your choices are the strokes on the canvas.

At death, this canvas
will either be a treasured masterpiece
or an unnoticed scribbling.

That would be the judgement day
on how good a painter you were
in painting your life.

• • •

Pampering weakens you.
Love creates you.

It seems, 'the need to be pampered', rather than 'the need to be loved', is the greatest craving. What's the difference? To a lot of people, being loved means their loved ones should always be soft with them, always agree with what they say, never complain or criticise, never push them beyond their comfort zones... basically leave them as they are, and not show any signs of wanting to change them. Pampering is - love me only the way I want to be loved.

Love is not love that pampers. Love is love that makes a difference. Pampering weakens you. Love creates you.

No man is perfect. There is endless scope to improve. Except those who love you, no one else cares about whether you improve or not. In the name of tolerance, pampering will leave you with your imperfections. Even at the cost of hurting your ego, love will give you feedback to make a difference to you. Pampering works on your ego. Love works on you.

No man can always be right. In the name of acceptance, pampering will make what's not okay look okay. Love will act as a mirror and reflect you to you - not as you want to be seen, but as you truly are. Pampering is a mere façade, wanting to appear nice. Love will take the risk of being mistaken and yet be a constructive critic.

The motivation levels of most people are low. You need someone or something outside of you to push you. Pampering will sinfully leave you in your low-performing, comfort zone. Love will even dare to risk the friendship to create the friend. To demand - 'Give more of yourself to life' is an intense expression of love. You cannot be left as you are. That which does not change does not grow. The call to awaken one from his slumber is pure, classic love.

Pampering is like boozing. It gives you a joyful evening, but nothing about you will change. Love is like meditation. It may seem like nothing is happening and yet everything about you will change. Crave to be loved and to be created, and not to be pampered and allowed to stagnate.

Oh my beloved! I say to you, "My love may not come to you in the packaging you want. However, my love serves a purpose. It will create you."

• • •

Acceptance = Positive Emotion

When someone is doing something in a way I don't want it to be done and I am not able to accept it, I become angry. However, when someone is doing something in a way I don't want it to be done but I am able to accept it, I remain tolerant.

When someone has something that I don't have, or someone is able to produce results that I am not able to produce and I am not able to accept it, I become jealous. However, if I can accept it, I get inspired.

When I encounter uncertainty and I am not sure about how I am going to handle it, and I am not able to accept it - it causes fear in me. When I encounter uncertainty and I am not sure about how I am going to handle it, but I am able to accept it - I feel adventurous.

When someone has done something that has emotionally hurt me and I am not able to accept it, it develops hatred in me. When someone has done something that has emotionally hurt me and I am able to accept it, it helps me forgive them.

When someone is present in my thoughts but is not physically present, and I am not able to accept it, I say 'I am missing you'. When someone is present in my thoughts but is not physically present, and I am able to accept it, I say 'I am thinking of you'.

Then, the emotional equation is quite simple.

Something + Acceptance   = Positive Emotion

Something + Non-acceptance = Negative Emotion

So, it is not 'something' or 'someone' who is making me feel positive or negative, but it is my 'acceptance' or 'non-acceptance' of something or someone that is making me feel positive or negative. It isn't the world, but the quality of my response to the world (acceptance or non-acceptance) that determines the quality of my emotions.

The next time I find myself disturbed by a negative emotion, instead of asking who or what is disturbing me, I will examine who or what I am resisting (not accepting). I will replace resistance (non-acceptance) with acceptance, and the negative emotion will turn into a positive one.

Emotional management begins by stopping to blame that 'something' or 'someone' and starting to take the responsibility to respond to life with 'acceptance'.

Knowledge is given to you not to dissect your past but to construct your future.

With chapters and chapters of failure and 19 years of mediocre living behind me, I listened to my friend Vijayaraghavan telling me: "The harder you press the spring, the faster it will bounce back when you release it. So what if your life has been filled with failures for 19 years? Decide to bounce back now. Rewrite your script." It was my very first awakening, and ever since I haven't looked back in life... there has been no need to. I'm glad I didn't tell Vijayaraghavan, "If only you had come into my life with this message five years ago!"

What is important is, at the point of knowledge, where are you looking - are you looking at your past or are you looking at your future?

I can either say, 'My English isn't good', or say, 'I want to make my English better'. Stand on your today and look at your tomorrow, not at your yesterday. At the point of

---

knowledge don't look back, look ahead. People who use the language 'If only...' are fundamentally people who, at the point of knowledge, are looking at their past. You are awakened to build your future; don't try in vain to renovate your past.

No knowledge ever comes to you late... it comes to you when it has to come... when you are ready for it. The same message from Vijayaraghavan a few years earlier would have had no bearing on me. Never question existential timing.

When Mohandas Karamchand Gandhi looks ahead, a Mahatma Gandhi happens. When Narendra looks ahead, a Swami Vivekananda happens. Our future is not equivalent to our past. The greatest motivation to look forward to our tomorrow is in the realisation that 'Our best is yet to come'. With every piece of knowledge, with every new realisation, with every profound awakening... let us progress to build our desired future.

Knowledge is never given to you to dissect your past. It is given to you to construct your future.

Look ahead... you never know what you may become. Somewhere in the future, the person you are going to become is already waiting for you. Go... go and meet the person you shall be.

• • •

Quality is that invisible detail.

I was shocked to see the celebrated speaker get out of his dirty car... so dirty that I wouldn't even touch it with gloves on my left hand... the inside of the car was the closest I have seen to a garbage chute... the speaker was going to deliver a lecture on 'Quality of Life'. Hmmm... I have seen disciples walking out of a spiritual satsang, cleaning the dirt in their eyes... a confirmation that people who don't even care about the cleanliness of their bodies seek the cleansing of their souls... what ignorance! They don't even bathe, but they want their lives to be bathed by the grace of their Guru. I have seen sales personnel with unshaven faces, unpolished shoes, badly worn ties, screaming their sales pitch on the 'World-class Quality' of their products and services.

We ought to realise that quality begins on the inside and then works its way out. The quality of what we give depends on the quality of what we have; the

---

quality of what we have depends on the quality of what we do; and the quality of what we do depends on the quality of what we are.

Quality consciousness is expecting more from yourself than what anyone else expects of you. Quality consciousness is setting higher standards for yourself than what the world has set for you. Quality consciousness is the belief that everything can and must be improved.

Quality is about not having a hole in your socks... no creaking doors... all the clocks in the house showing the same time... no torn upholstery... no dirty fans, no cobwebs on the wall, no leaking taps... the phone picked up within five rings... no surfaces with the paint peeling off... staff washrooms so clean that one can actually lie down on the floor... door latches that work...

Quality - the presence of which is seldom noticed, but the absence of which can never be missed. Quality is about detailed excellence in areas that others might not even notice... A flower is a flower, with or without the fragrance; yet the presence of the fragrance makes all the difference. Quality is that invisible detail... the presence of which makes all the difference.

• • •

Everybody has an explanation
for everything and everybody
wants to have the last word.

My friend was convinced that I was wrong. She had an explanation as to why she thought so. I clarified to her as to why I had done what I had done. I had an explanation as to why I felt I wasn't wrong. She had an explanation as to why she thought my explanation did not justify my point. She explained further as to why I was still wrong. I explained how she hadn't taken my explanation in the right spirit. I explained further as to why I was still right... she was bent on proving me wrong and I was bent on proving myself right. Both of us had enough explanations to substantiate our points of view.

He sends an email criticising me and I reply to deny the accusation... he replies to substantiate his view and I give an explanation as to why I don't agree to it...

I have realised two things... everybody has an explanation for everything, and more importantly, everybody wants to have the last word.

Nathuram Godse had an explanation for having assassinated Mahatma Gandhi. Osama Bin Laden has an explanation as to why he led the terrorist attack on the World Trade Centre. Actors have their explanation as to why they think it's okay for them to smoke on screen. My wife has an explanation for having forgotten to add salt in the *sambar* and I have my explanation as to why my anger is justified.

Everybody has an explanation and everybody wants to have the last word. In fact, the realisation that I have been trying to explain myself for everything, and that I have been trying to have the 'last word' all my life is indeed a little embarrassing, to say the least.

I have told myself that on all the inconsequential issues of life, I will consciously allow the other person to have the last word and save myself a lot of time, energy, effort and space. There is enormous freedom in curtailing this instinct of offering an explanation and letting the other have the 'last word'... of course, on all the inconsequential issues of life. Fortunately, more than 90% of all issues are inconsequential.

Do you have a different point of view on this? You are entitled to it. I have nothing to say. You can have the last word.

● ● ●

'10 minutes early' means
I can live 10 years longer.

There are two ways of catching a flight. If you've been flying regularly, then chances are you belong to this most common category. Getting stressed at the pace of traffic movement, driving the driver to drive a little faster, thinking of jumping signals, repeatedly glancing at your watch and rushing into the airport. In every queue from baggage scanning to check-in to the security check, trying to jump the queue by explaining to everyone that you are running a little late for your flight... Walking a little faster to start with and then maybe even jogging to make it... a tense face, yet managing a smile for every attendant to make a case for yourself... finally, you barely make it to the flight.

The second way is to leave for the airport 10 minutes early.

There are two ways that a morning can start in every home. The first way is to simulate World War III. Everyone is running... Everyone delegates work to everyone else... The phone is ringing and everyone is hoping that someone else will pick it up. Someone's at

---

the door and everyone is pretending not to have heard the doorbell. The school bus must have already turned round the corner of the road... where is the lunch box... here, take the water bottle, the school bag is not closed properly, get into the bus and tie your shoelace... it looks like a rocket launch... 10... 9... 8... Hmmm....

The other way is to wake up 10 minutes early.

Urgency is the most dangerous of all addictions. It forces us to take decisions that we'd rather not take. It forces us to act in ways that we'd rather not. It cheats us by making us believe that the situation is at fault, and not us. Urgency becomes an excuse for shoddy work and sloppy decision-making. It creates an atmosphere in which we tend to justify everything we do - from jumping queues to running like fools to catch a flight.

Difficult decisions are often good decisions. '10 minutes early' will seem foolish to begin with, but it is the antidote to present-day neurosis. '10 minutes early' is one big medicine for most stress-related issues today's man faces. '10 minutes early' will ensure that you will not have time for an appointment with crisis.

'10 minutes early' means my heart can slow down by 10 counts... so that I can live 10 years longer.

●●●

Dreams are the gap between where you are and where you will be.

Martin Luther King, Jr. delivered a historic speech when he stated, "I have a dream that one day this nation will rise up and live out the true meaning of its creed: 'We hold these truths to be self-evident, that all men are created equal.' I have a dream that one day on the red hills of Georgia, the sons of former slaves and the sons of former slave owners will be able to sit down together at the table of brotherhood. I have a dream that my four little children will one day live in a nation where they will not be judged by the colour of their skin but by the content of their character. I have a dream today! With this faith, we will be able to work together, to pray together, to struggle together, to go to jail together, to stand up for freedom together, knowing that we will be free one day. And if America is to be a great nation, this must become true." Four decades later, the American nation did make history by electing their first Afro-American President in Barack Obama.

What is very significant here is that this dream was not implanted into the social consciousness during the best of times but during the worst of times, when the blacks didn't even have voting rights.

Dhirubhai Ambani dreamt of a digital India, where the common man would have access to affordable means of information and communication, which would in turn help him overcome the handicaps of illiteracy and mobility. It did become a reality in India. What is significant here is that this dream was implanted into the mind of Reliance's intelligentsia in 1999, when basic communication channels were still quite dismal in India. With every product, service and commodity becoming more and more expensive, a Ratan Tata dreamt of a one-lakh-rupee car and through 'Nano' he turned his dream into reality.

Mahatma Gandhi dreamt of a free India at a time when the country was already enslaved and in the clutches of foreign rulers for well over three centuries. At a time when India could not even build world-class aircrafts, the man popularly known as the 'Missile Man of India', APJ Abdul Kalam, dreamt, "In the 3000-year history of India, barring 600 years, the country has been ruled by others. If you need development, the country should witness peace and peace is ensured by strength." Missiles were developed to strengthen the country. India placed itself both in 'space' and on the 'moon'.

Dream we must, that all of us know. What is significant here is that all these great dreamers processed great dreams not just during the best of times but even during the toughest of times, during very difficult times, during times when the collective social consciousness wasn't optimistic. Yet, dream they did, and on the sheer strength of their dreams, organisations, nations and humanity as a whole stood up.

Difficult times you may face. Tough times you may encounter. But, dream you must. Dreams are the gap between where you are and where you will be. "Will I?" is never the question. Great dreams of great dreamers will always be fulfilled. Whatever the mind of a man can conceive and believe, it can achieve. God never gives you an idea without the power to achieve it. For a dreamer, the question is just, "By when will I?"

• • •

What water can do, gasoline cannot.
What copper can, gold cannot.

The fragility of the ant
enables it to move.
The rigidity of the tree
enables it to stay rooted.

Everything and everybody
has been designed with a proportion of
uniqueness to serve a purpose.

How can I be anyone other than me,
even if I have my share of weaknesses?
Why should I struggle to be someone else,
even if someone's strengths appeal to me?

I am here to be I.

• • •

Consistent and
never-ending
self-improvement
is the only way.

I wasn't good at writing even compositions or essays at school. However, as an orator, I have been gifted with this rare ability to present even the most complex wisdom in the simplest of forms. I can conceptualise even the most intriguing truths of life and teach them in a language that anyone can understand. Basically, I have content value on life and living. So I decided to give writing a shot. But who would publish my writing? So I decided to publish a magazine. That's how Frozen Thoughts came into existence.

The first time I wrote for Frozen Thoughts in the year 2000, I must confess that even I didn't enjoy reading my own article. Soon I realised my English grammar wasn't good either. A reader hurled the first issue of Frozen Thoughts at me and screamed, "Disgusting and complex sentence formations. Lousy language, terrible grammar, cheap jokes, gaudy colour combinations and hundreds of spelling mistakes... this magazine is worth my foot." Hurt can be a major source of inspiration, and to me it was. If you throw a dagger at me, I will catch it by the handle and not by the blade. Now, that dagger becomes an additional weapon in my arsenal. A situation becomes an opportunity when the resources you have are greater than the situation you face. I saw an opportunity. Luck is the meeting point of all opportunities that pass by you and your alertness to grab them. I decided to author my luck. So I put a team together to overcome these issues. You don't have to be all that intelligent, if you know how to surround yourself with enough intelligent people. I built an intelligent team around me. You need to know the subject to lead people in the subject. So I started working on my writing, got back to learning the fundamentals of grammar, set out to learn design and technology - did everything that was needed to qualify myself for the responsibility.

I am not saying that editing, publishing and distributing a magazine is very complicated, but I found it complicated because I didn't have the requisites to execute the responsibilities. A situation is considered a challenge when the situation you face is larger than the resources you have. My plight was that I had a challenge at hand. I wasn't good enough for the chair I assumed. So, I had to commit myself to consistent and never-ending self-improvement. I got better at everything I had to get better at.

There are no stagnant responsibilities... they are dynamic. So, your personal growth has to keep pace with it. Being the editor is not a crown given to me, but a responsibility that I have undertaken. Today, Frozen Thoughts enjoys global readership in over 65 countries and in over 450 locations in India. Today, it is heart-warming to know that nobody will throw a copy of Frozen Thoughts. It is even more gratifying to know that this 'Unposted Letter' book you are holding in your hand is born from the womb of Frozen Thoughts.

Today's challenge is that the role a person assumes is growing faster than the person. Efficiency and effectiveness happens when man keeps up with the pace of growth of his roles. Consistent and never-ending self-improvement is the only way.

• • •

Nobody succeeds all the time.
Nobody is destined to remain a failure either.

Success is failure delayed
and failure is success delayed.
Neither is failure final
nor is success permanent.

Today's success and today's failures
are just another step in the long journey
of life. Life is a game. If you play this
game long enough, you will make it.

Don't quit midway.
Play to the end. Play it long enough.
Eventually, you will cross the finishing line.

When was the last time
I did something for
the first time?

For most people, life is a repetitive drill. Waking up at the same time, struggling in bed for a few minutes before getting up, brushing the same way, drinking the same coffee, reading the same newspaper, a time bound bath, a hurried breakfast, road rage on the way to work, same office, same work, gossip and lunch, same talk, same route back home, same mega serials, same arguments, compulsive dinner, same bed, crash out and wake up another time to another day to the same drill.

Life needn't be mundane. Life needn't be boring. Life needn't be a year's experience repeated 'n' times. Life needn't be an imposition. Life needn't be a life imprisonment. There's more to life than existing.

Pursue a new proficiency every year and see how exciting life can be. Let there not be a phase in your life when you aren't enrolled as an active student. It could be music lessons, playing instruments, dance classes, alternative medicine, new fitness regimes, yoga, new languages, advanced grammar, creative writing, public speaking, cooking classes, painting, handwriting, new art forms, driving, swimming, a new sport, technical education, spiritual study groups, gardening, raising pet birds and animals, keeping an aquarium, photography, culture... the list is truly endless. Choose any and remain an active student.

Always be an explorer of life. Keep experimenting. Keep trying. Feed your curiosity and inquisitiveness. Keep attempting something that hasn't been attempted before. Try out new cuisines. Wear clothes you are shy of wearing. Try a new hairstyle. Visit unusual places. Men, run the kitchen for a day. Have a husbands' get-together on a Sunday and serve the wives. Spend a day blindfolded. Go on voice rest another day. Use public transport for a day. Switch roles at your workplace - how about the MD at the reception for a day? Again, the list is endless. Get creative with life. Keep going.

More than all your successes, achievements and accomplishments, the formula to a lively life is to keep answering this question: When was the last time I did something for the first time?

Celebrate life. Stamp your presence on every day of your life. Spell life with L.I.F.E. Be excited to be alive.

• • •

Less will make it long.
More will make it short.

I t is a commonly observed phenomenon to see organisations grow very fast and then crumble even faster than that. Ask people who have burnt their fingers in the stock market by investing on such companies and the hordes of others who've lost all their money on such finance companies... they will have tearful tales to tell you.

Of course, it is also not uncommon to see organisations that take time to build their base, establish business models, get their fundamentals right, put systems and infrastructure in place. These organisations, though slow in their initial progress, keep growing in geometric progression over the years. Ask people who have amassed assets by investing on such technically sound companies... they will have success stories to tell you.

'Rome was not built in a day,' goes the saying. If Rome was built in a day, it would have fallen the next day.

Even in the case of relationships, I have observed that relationships where people get obsessed with each other within a short span of time, break up over a single misunderstanding, a single incident, a single argument. Only relationships that gain strength, confidence, transparency and intimacy over a period of time, develop the stability and depth required to stand the test of time.

Which will have greater stability - a cone standing on its base or an inverted cone? It takes time to set the base right. Might as well invest time in the beginning to get the base right rather than spending time later to keep correcting the mess.

You say, "I like eating." Precisely for the same reason, eat less. Then you will live long enough to eat. You say, "I like sleeping." Precisely for the same reason, sleep less. Then you will live long enough to sleep. You say, "I love him a lot." Precisely for the same reason, give him space. You say, "I want to hit the top." Precisely for the same reason, invest enough time at the bottom to build the base. Then the base will sustain you at the top.

Less will make it long. More will make it short.

Where there is excellence, explanations are not required.

Excellence is self-explanatory. Where there is excellence, explanations are not required. Where explanations are required, rarely do you find excellence.

What's okay is okay and what's not okay is not okay. However, we have a tendency to explain, justify, reason and rationalise what's not okay as okay. Hold it. Once you develop this tendency of using your mind to make what's not okay look okay, you press your own self-destruction button. The mind that gets trained into justifying lack of excellence learns to settle for compromises - it learns to live with compromises.

If you have scored 88 out of 100, the fact remains that you have fallen short by 12. How much ever you explain, you've still fallen short by 12. Communication cannot make up for the 12. You are attempting to justify 88 as 100, though you yourself know that 88 is only 88.

A saying goes, 'A lie told a thousand times becomes the truth'. To others, it may appear to be the truth but you will always know that it is a lie. For how long can you make a cat look like a lion? You can neither hide the fact from yourself, nor hide yourself from the fact. Explanations can never make up for the shortfall.

If your target was 40 lakhs and you did only 36 lakhs, then you've fallen short of your target. If your appointment was at 11.00 and you turned up only at 11.15, then you are late. Much after you have explained everything in every possible way, the fact remains that you didn't achieve your target, and that you didn't respect punctuality.

Self-consolation for lack of excellence will hurt you very badly in life. Time and again, it will make you fall short of the mark and you will eventually fall short of what you are capable of. Wake up. What's not okay is not okay. 6.01 is not 6.00; Monday alone is Monday.

'Zero defect' is possible. Precision is possible. Sustained excellence is possible. It all starts with the attitude of refusing to settle for anything but the best. It's a funny thing about life that if you refuse to settle for anything but the best, it often gives it to you.

Lack of excellence should hurt. That which hurts, instructs. That which instructs, creates. Get created. Create excellence. Let your work speak for you. You don't speak for it.

●●●

Information has become
the basis of trust,
and hence
the basis of relationships.

"I have never questioned my parents. Whatever they asked me to do was simply done. I have unquestioned respect for my parents. But my son isn't like that. Whenever I ask him to do something, I have to answer his 'Why, What, How and Why not'. Children of this generation don't respect elders," complains a middle-aged man.

It isn't true. It's just that the framework of relationships has changed. In the yesteryears, emotions formed the basis of relationships. Today, the basis of relationships is information.

A few years back, if the boss asked a team member to carry out a task, 'Done' would have been the spontaneous reply. Today, the team member asks the boss - "Why should it be done, what for, etc..." before doing it. This doesn't mean that today's team members are disrespectful, but just that they need to be adequately informed. In that sense, unquestioned surrender is no more there in relationships. But I still believe that the quality of relationships hasn't undergone any degradation whatsoever. It's just that today's intelligence says - either give me all the information to make a decision, or give me all the information that has led to the decision that I have to abide by.

You would've fetched water for your father at the slightest hint, but your son will ask you a few questions before doing the same for you - what's important is that he too brings water for you after he's been given sufficient information. The parent-child relationship in that sense has not degraded; it's just that the framework of the relationship has changed. When Dad called Mom to tell her that three more people would be joining him for lunch, she would've simply said okay. If you happen to communicate the same to your wife, she'll ask you who's coming, at what time, what their preferences are, till what time they'll stay... but then, she too keeps the food ready. In that sense, the devotion in marriage hasn't degraded; it's just that the framework of the relationship has changed... the basis of relationships has changed from emotions to information.

As a teacher, I don't think the quality of surrender has changed even in the realm of spirituality. This is the change that has happened - it has changed from unquestioned surrender to surrender after enough questions and answers. But then, was Arjuna any different?

The quality of relationships hasn't degraded, but the demands on communication and information have gone up. Communication and exchange of information have become the lifeline for relationships. Explanations have become necessary, and clarifications mandatory. This change is neither for the better nor for the worse; it's just a new phenomenon. In a changing world, such changes have to be anticipated. It's no more enough to say 'Do'. Explain enough, then say 'Do', and it will be done.

Trust is the basis of relationships, but trust is no more assumed. Information has become the basis of trust, and hence the basis of relationships.

• • •

All relationships are only on the surface.
Deep inside you are always alone.

A thousand people may surround you;
yet, a part of you is always alone.
Even when you embrace your beloved,
a part of you is always alone.

You came into this world alone
and you will leave this world alone.

Liberation comes from knowing
'Existential Aloneness'
is your true nature.

Relate from this space
and you will be dependable;
else, you will be dependant.

What the world calls failure, I call it a turning point.

At 17, I aspired to become an engineer but owing to the marks I scored in my 12th standard, I could only do graduation in Mathematics. As mere graduation did not promise a bright future, I had to pursue additional courses in computer programming. What I wanted and what happened were two different things, but so what? By the age of 25, I started my own software consultancy and had many engineers and MCAs working with me. At 17, when I couldn't achieve a desired consequence, the world called me a failure. But in reality, it was this unintended consequence that shaped me into a success.

All my long-term goals were related only to Information Technology, and yet for totally unintended reasons, I founded Alma Mater when I was 30 and then Frozen Thoughts when I was 35... I couldn't continue in the direction of my goals, but life pulled me in unintended directions to reveal the very purpose of my life.

Agnes Gonxha Bojaxhiu of Yugoslavia, came to India to teach in a convent school in Calcutta - unintended, the heart of Mother Teresa was revealed to the world. Balakrishna Menon, an editorial staff of 'The National Herald', who always believed that all *sadhus* were one big bluff, approached Swami Sivananda to write an article - unintended, a Swami Chinmayananda was revealed to the world. After all, the discovery of America was, for Christopher Columbus, an unintended consequence.

People who have achieved great heights through unintended consequences have made greater impact on the world than those who had set their goals and achieved them.

So, if you don't get what you want in life, if after all your efforts, the results don't turn out to be what you aspired for, if the consequences of your choices are not what you intended, don't lose heart.

Unintended consequences are life's way of showing you the possibilities you haven't thought about. Unintended consequences are Existence's way of telling you that it has a different plan for you... a plan larger than what you intended. God upsets your plans sometimes to execute His plans for you.

What the world calls failure, I call it a turning point.

• • •

Speak the negative in two sentences and say at least five sentences about the positive.

Our subconscious seeks depth of emotions. The subconscious choice is never between positive emotions and negative emotions, but between deep emotions and shallow emotions. Since negative emotions always enjoy greater attention than the positive ones, most human beings sink into the depth of negative emotions with effortless ease. Alternatively, they are very shallow in experiencing their positive emotions. Take your own case and think about it!

The child is happily playing in the house. The rest of us are lost in our own chores. The happiness of the child never attracts deep attention. However, when the child hurts herself, every family member comes towards the child asking, "What happened?" Unaware, we program the subconscious of the child into believing that her crying draws more attention than her happiness. In the future, even after she grows into an adult, whenever she wants attention she will sink into some form of crying - from tears to depression to tantrums - the range varies. Her emotions will seem so legitimate to her, though others may notice the incongruence of it. This is a subconscious choice, and not a conscious one. She won't even be aware that something within her (her subconscious) is choosing not only her emotions, but also the life situations to suit those emotions. A subconscious craving for deep emotions is driving her.

Between deep hatred and shallow love, your subconscious will always choose hatred. That's why you can process hurt and hatred for years, and yet, every few days you need renewals of expressions of love. Else, it hurts. See the irony! You are self-sufficient when it comes to keeping your hatred alive, but need external help to keep your love going. The remedy is to learn to experience deep love. Intensify your expressions and demonstrations of love. Sink in love.　Drown in love.　Epitomise love.　More importantly, learn to tranquilise hurt and hatred with forgiveness and keep it shallow.　Eventually, your subconscious will spontaneously choose love over hatred, for the sheer depth of it.　It will also begin to choose life situations in congruence with love.

Learn from your failures and leave it at that.　Don't get too emotional about it.　Don't spoil your subconscious. Celebrate your success.　Get every cell of yours involved.　Pamper your subconscious.　Ill health deserves nothing more than a passing remark.　Oh, brag about your health and fitness.　Let your subconscious know your preference.

The solution is simple.　Speak the negative in two sentences and say at least five sentences about the positive.　Ration your emotions to the negative and create an emotional flood for the positive.　That's transformation - TRANScending the old FORMATION of the subconscious into a new one.

Someone said a sad heart writes the most beautiful poetry.　So, God must have been sad when he created this beautiful world.　Oh, then he hasn't seen my God. Learn to experience the depth of bliss.　You will no more need to write poetry.　It will simply happen through you. Your very life will become poetry.

●●●

Why do we lie?

*We lie because it helps us to escape a
situation which may not be pleasant.*

*The curse of lying is that
it develops in us the 'attitude to escape'.
The blessing of honesty is that
it develops in us the 'attitude to face'.*

*If you want to hit the top
you need the 'attitude to face'
everything in life.*

*And, what will shape this attitude in you?
Honesty!*

● ● ●

It doesn't matter if you don't have all the answers.
Do you have the
right questions?

The seeker asked, "Why do bad things happen to good people?" The Pastor replied, "When the question itself is wrong, how do you expect me to answer it? The question should have been, 'What happens to good people when bad things happen to them' and the reply would be, 'They become better people'!"

It is not our intelligence, but it is the direction of our intelligence that determines the pace of our progress. And, our intelligence can be directed, if only we know how to ask the right questions. Ask, "Why me?" for all your troubles and listen to the response of your intelligence. Again ask, "Why me?" for all those countless blessings and again listen to the voice of your intelligence. Note the difference. Experience the power of questions. Questions have great power. One right question asked at the right time can change the direction of our intelligence, and thus change the direction of our life.

"Why is this happening to me?" sets your intelligence in a direction that will lead you to self-pity. In the same scenario ask, "What can I learn from this?" and it will direct you to higher maturity. "Why she does not understand me?" will lead your intelligence to blame the other and also make you feel victimised. Instead try "What should be my approach to make her understand me?" and you will feel you are still in control of the situation. It puts you in a more resourceful and responsible position.

If you are feeling stagnant, if you are not growing at the pace at which you can grow, if you are going in the direction that will not lead you to your goals, if you are encountering issues that are repetitive in nature, then you can be sure that you are not asking the right questions. Hence, you are not directing your intelligence right.

Simple questions like - 'What next', 'How can I do what I am already doing even better', 'What is the worst that can possibly happen' can completely change the way you perceive life. Our intelligence has an inherent compulsion to answer any question that is posed to it, either by you or by the world. So, choose your questions and direct your intelligence in constructive ways.

Isidor Isaac Rabi, a physicist and Nobel laureate, recognised for his discovery of nuclear magnetic resonance said, "My mother made me a scientist without ever intending to. Every other Jewish mother in Brooklyn would ask her child after school, 'So, did you learn anything today?' But not my mother. 'Izzy', she would say, 'did you ask a good question today?' That difference - asking good questions, made me a scientist."

One man asked, "Why is the apple falling down?" and the world has not been the same ever since. In fact, all inventions and discoveries begin with a question. Arjuna with his questions gave a direction to Krishna's intelligence, which we know as the Bhagavad-Gita.

It doesn't matter if you don't have all the answers. What truly matters is - do you have the right questions? Your intelligence is waiting... Ask and you shall receive.

• • •

Even if no one believes in you,
you got to believe in yourself.
Even if no one believes you can,
you got to believe you can.
You will believe in yourself,
only when you learn to love yourself.

So, even if no one loves you,
you got to love yourself.
In fact, only when
you learn to love yourself,
the world will begin to love you.

All-in-all, how the world sees you
will make only a small difference to you,
but how you see yourself will make
all the difference to you.

● ● ●

Everybody is watching.

How long are we going to pacify ourselves by saying, 'but for his smoking, and chewing habits, my father is a great man'. How long are we going to satisfy ourselves by saying let us not look at the character of our teacher - that's his personal life; let us just take the teachings and leave it at that.

I am no global judge to decide what is right and what is wrong. I also know there are no universal rights and wrongs. Who am I to infringe into anybody's freedom of choice? But ask yourself the courageous question, "Will I be happy if my children take up what I think is okay for me? Will I ever be able to say that I am proud of myself, for I have these habits? Are my character traits worthy of emulation? Is my life an example or a warning to the next generation - not selectively, but holistically?"

Our children are watching us all the time. They learn much more by what they see than what they hear. Moral science is never learnt from books, but from watching those who live around us. The world will follow your example and not your advice.

The truth is that once a master has attained silence, he has attained the object of meditation and thus no longer requires the *sadhana*. But the ignorant seeker would argue, "When the master does not meditate regularly, I needn't either." The Bhagawad-Gita therefore reminds us - "Whatever a great man does, others will imitate. Whatever standards he sets, the world will follow." We've got to do certain things for the sake of inspiring others, irrespective of our reasoning. We have a social responsibility. We have to be a worthy role model. Do what must be done, and stop doing what shouldn't be done.

As a teacher, a boss, a pioneer in the industry, a parent, as the head of the family, one holding the government office... you, me, all of us have to live in ways that set standards for others to follow. Think, talk, act, and live the way you want others to think, talk, act and live. We cannot expect anything from the world that we are not willing to expect from ourselves.

Over a period of time, the world around you tends to become a carbon copy of you. Then for sure, you need to be a master-copy worth duplicating.

Mark Twain said, "Dance like nobody's watching."

I wish to tell you, "Live as though everybody is watching."

• • •

There is more to education than just academics.

S wami Vivekananda said, "Education is not the amount of information that is put into your brain and runs riot there, undigested, all your life. We must have life-building, man-making, character-making assimilation of ideas. If you have assimilated five ideas and made them your life and character, you have more education than any man who has got by heart a whole library. We want that education by which character is formed, strength of mind is increased, the intellect is expanded, and by which one can stand on one's own feet."

Somehow we have misunderstood academics to be education. From parents to teachers, everybody's focus has tilted too much towards academics. What will a child do with science, if he doesn't understand the science of life? We teach our children to read and memorise history, but we don't teach them to create history. What will a child do with her first and second and third languages, if her communication skills are not developed?

Let me not be misunderstood. I am not saying that academics is nothing; I am only asserting that academics alone does not complete education. Academics is one aspect of a child's development, and not the only aspect. Academics will aid life, but academics alone is not life. There is more to life. Every first-rank holder does not necessarily come first in life, and not all backbenchers have remained backbenchers in life. In fact, we often see a '98% with an average understanding of life' eventually working for a '72% with a comprehensive understanding of life'.

Relationships are the very fabric of life. Communication is the lifeline of relationships. Success is all about leadership - you will either lead or will be led. Where your time goes, there your future comes. So, time management skills, in essence, are life management skills. You can either be dependable or dependent, and that depends on your self-image. The sad fact is that none of the above mentioned life-essentials is part of our academic system.

So please, parents, teachers and other custodians of our children's future, let us not confine our children to a syllabus. Let us expose them to life, and of course, also to academics. Let us not only count their marks, but also, make their life count.

• • •

There is no way to happiness.
Happiness is the way.

When work is done as a choice, you tend to enjoy what you do; and when it is finally completed, you experience a sense of fulfilment. That which gives you fulfilment, you look forward to doing again and again and again...

On the contrary, when work is undertaken as a compulsion, you struggle to do what you do; and when it is finally completed, you only experience a sense of relief. That which gives you relief, you want to avoid in the future. Even if you do it again, you will only do it reluctantly.

People who do everything as a choice are always fulfiled in life and hence they thirst for more and more of life. People who do everything as a compulsion are tired of living and hence they even go to the extent of desiring to be relieved from life.

People have become reluctant even to carry out their daily chores... People have become reluctant to cook... haven't precooked foods, fast foods, frozen foods and ready-made foods invaded every kitchen?

People are becoming reluctant to sit and enjoy their meal... isn't skipping breakfast and not finding time for lunch becoming common? Adults are becoming more reluctant to go to work than their children to school... how else can you explain the increase in the number of heart attacks on Monday mornings?

If everything essential about life is seen as a compulsion, and if everything is completed with a sigh of relief... how can we improve the quality of our life?

Please, let's add celebration to everything we do. Let us shift from the attitude of 'I must do it; I should do it' to 'I WANT to do it'. Let every action of ours start as a choice, be filled with enjoyment and end in fulfilment. If something has to anyhow be done, we might as well enjoy doing it.

The disciple asked, "Master, before enlightenment and after enlightenment, you are only drawing water from the well and chopping woods. There seems to be no difference in your actions!" The Master said, "Oh, there is no difference in my actions, but the quality with which I perform my actions has changed."

Confucius so apltly said, "Choose a job you love, and you will never have to work a day in your life."

There is no way to happiness. Happiness is the way.

Without God,
I cannot.

Without me,
God will not.

God plus me
anything is possible.

● ● ●

Man judges my actions.
God judges my intentions.

A boy and a girl embraced each other. After some time when I had a chance to speak to them, one said, 'I experienced sisterly affection in embracing her,' and the other said, 'I think he is the man of my life'. The action performed by both was the same, but the intentions were not.

When one kills another in a war, he becomes a national hero; but when one kills another within a nation, he is called a killer. To murder is a crime; to hang the murderer by a court order is a hangman's duty. When one gives his life for the sake of the nation, he becomes a martyr; but when one ends his own life by committing suicide, he is termed a coward. The thief uses a knife; the surgeon also uses a knife.

There is no sin in action; the sin is always in the intention behind the action.

Understanding this eases relationships. It makes it easier for you to practice forgiveness; it helps you mould people; and most importantly, it enables you to put everything about people in proper perspective. Personally, it has helped me to see almost all people around me thro' positive eyes. Though their actions weren't always right, I was able to see that the intentions behind their actions, weren't always wrong.

However, I need to be aware that the world around me will continue to judge me only by my actions. That's why the results you produce through your actions always score over the nobility of the intentions with which you work. That's why even when you know that people love you, you still need to hear it from them. That's why we end up having to explain ourselves time and again even to people who we believe know us better than the palm of their own hands.

While we should view the world with the understanding that 'There is no sin in action; the sin is always in the intention behind the action', we should also be aware that the world will judge us only by our actions... irrespective of what our intentions are.

While Existence may punish or reward us based on our intentions, man will punish or reward us only based on our actions. Shall we strive to be good at both and win both the worlds? Able actions backed up by noble intentions is the way of a complete man.

● ● ●

What you don't use,
you lose.

I have seen people, who were extraordinary public
speakers, struggle to stamp the same mark on the
dais a few years later, for they've lost touch with
public speaking. I have seen well-educated women,
who after having become homemakers confined
themselves to the four walls, struggle with their
fluency in communication. I have seen outstanding
singers unable to achieve the level of performance
they are capable of, for they have stopped practicing.

Why is it that I am not able to exert my left hand as
much as my right hand? Simple, I have put my right
hand to greater use than my left hand. You develop the
muscles you use and lose the ones you don't use. Most
cardiac problems are the result and effect of the heart
not being made to work to its maximum capacity. The
heart that is made to work keeps working. So is the
case with every part of your body... The human body
is designed to wear out over a lifetime, but we shrink
this lifetime by allowing the body to rust.

If you don't use it, you lose it.

Unused money devalues. Unused talent diminishes. Unused potential decays. Unused machinery gets rusted. Unused time dies. Unused knowledge becomes a burden. What isn't used is abused.

It reminds me of the biblical parable of talents, where the master, before going on a journey, called his three servants and entrusted them with different talents. On the return of the master, the first servant said he had added five more talents to the five entrusted. The second servant said he had added two more talents to the two entrusted. The master was pleased and he told both of them, "You were faithful with a few things. So, I will put you in charge of many things." The third servant returned the only talent entrusted without using it, and the master said, "Take away the talent from him and give it to the one who has ten talents."

Matthew 25:29 states, "For, to everyone who has shall more be given, and he shall have abundance; but from the one who does not have, even what he does have shall be taken away."

The tragedy of life isn't the ultimate death, but the resources that die within you when you are still alive. Let us not die while we are still breathing.

Use it or you will lose it.

• • •

Show me your friends and I'll tell you who you are.

Just the previous morning, the little girl in office was as restless as running water while speaking about the purpose of her life, her future plans, goals and achievements. She was clear about how she wanted to utilise her time and potential. The next morning, not surprisingly though, she was only speaking about the latest movies that she hadn't seen, the pastries she hadn't eaten in a long time and how much she missed her window-shopping schedules. It isn't about what is right and what is wrong, but about what has changed in 24 hours. The company of people she kept the 'day before' and the people she met the 'next day' made all the difference.

The company of people you keep is a double-edged sword... it has both the power to create you and the power to destroy you. The company of people we surround ourselves with has a tremendous bearing on the way we think, the way we feel, the way we look at others, the way we look at ourselves, our present and the future we will create. True, there are people who have emerged 'in spite' of their surroundings... we aren't discussing exceptions; the majority of human minds are shaped by their environment... 'because' of their surroundings.

Your today is not simply shaped by your yesterday; your today is in many ways shaped by the people with whom you spent (or invested) your yesterday. Your tomorrow will be shaped by the people you give your today to.

A member of a certain church, who was a regular at service, suddenly stopped going. A few weeks later, the pastor decided to visit him. It was a chilly evening. The pastor found the man alone at home, sitting before a blazing fire. The man welcomed the pastor and led him to a big chair near the fireplace and waited. The pastor made himself comfortable, but said nothing. After a few minutes, the pastor took the tongs, carefully picked up a brightly glowing ember and kept it aside. Then he sat back in his chair, saying nothing.

The host watched in fascination. The glow of the lone ember slowly diminished, and soon it was cold and dead. Not a single word had been uttered since the initial greeting. Just before the pastor was ready to leave, he picked up the cold, dead ember and placed it back in the middle of the fire. Instantaneously, it began to glow once again with the light and heat of the burning coals around it. As the pastor prepared to leave, his host said, "Thank you so much for your visit, especially for the fiery sermon. I shall come back to church next Sunday."

He who walks with wise men will be wise, but the companion of fools will suffer harm - Proverbs 13:20.

They say an adopted child in due course of time becomes so much like the family into which he was adopted. True... we become like the company we keep. If we aren't growing at the pace at which we can and if we aren't living life with the grace and dignity with which we can, then we may have to make a bold decision... whether it is the organisation we work for, the company of people we relate to or the family in which we are growing... if it isn't creating us, we will have to shift ourselves to a different place from where we can grow. It is a tough decision, but a needed one too. What is the point in wasting a seed in a heap of garbage?

● ● ●

*Extraordinary people are ordinary people who
did everything with extraordinary passion.*

*Legendary living is in identifying a cause,
a cause that seems larger than your own life,
on which you are willing to invest
every breath of yours to the very last breath.*

*You make history,
when you have a cause that inspires you
to wake up every morning a little early
and keeps you awake a little late
and fills every minute in between
with the depths of passion.*

*In anything and everything give that 'extra'
and thus live an extraordinary life.*

• • •

Nothing is more powerful than an idea whose time has come.

A man keeps hanging from a scaffolding about 100 feet above the ground. He paints walls for his daily wages - that's his idea of 'making a living'. His counterpart has honed his painting skills a little and works on a contract basis - that's another idea of 'making a living'. Another has learnt to drive and has got himself employed as a driver in a businessman's house. He works for about 14 hours a day for a reasonable monthly salary - that's his idea of 'making a living'. A smarter one got himself employed as a driver in a corporate, thus entitling himself to other perks and benefits - that's another idea of 'making a living'. One uses his culinary skills to be employed as a cook in a house for a monthly salary, while another sets up his own roadside joint and earns his daily profits - they are both just different ideas of 'making a living'. Notice that all the above mentioned people have an idea of 'making a living' which does not presuppose any education or investment.

Your idea of 'making a living' could have been to be a salesman, his to be a software professional; her idea of 'making a living' could have been to be an entrepreneur, his to join the family business... of course, there are those who believe in the idea that there are no opportunities in this world to 'make a living'.

Let us realise that even the greatest of industrial enterprises were also once just an idea. Every revolution and every social organisation was once only an idea. This very book you are holding in your hand was once just an idea.

Nothing is more powerful than an idea whose time has come.

However, will that idea feed millions or just your own six-inch hunger pouch? Will the idea earn you a pittance or will it generate crores? It all depends on the mindset of the person in whose mind the idea is born, and what he does with that idea.

The bottom line is... you plus your idea can change your world...

● ● ●

With my loved ones,
I am what I always was.

˙

"The greatest of all fulfilments is to fill your life with accomplishments and then to be able to say, 'My results have not corrupted the core of my being. At the core, I am what I always was'. One of the greatest joys in life is to live life as a man above men, and yet walk as a man among the men. Let nothing of the outside touch the core of your inside." These were some of my concluding words at the annual spiritual retreat.

A few hours later, we arrived at the Mumbai airport. We were a group of 30 people. I happened to bump into an old friend with whom I had lost touch. It was almost a decade since we had met and he wasn't aware of the developments in my life. On hearing that we were returning from a spiritual retreat, he was overcome by a crazy thought. "Salute me and prove that you are still that same old friend," he said. Being the last person to be other-people conscious, I instantaneously saluted him. I know how much love and respect those 30 friends of mine have for me. So, I wasn't surprised to see expressions of deep hurt on their faces. However, it was a moment of great victory for my old friend. All he wanted was the same old friend, not some spiritually aligned being. The happiness I saw on his face said it all.

One day, my son called me up and asked me to take him out for dinner. I explained to him that it wouldn't be possible as I had to finish writing my regular column - 'Awakening', for Frozen Thoughts by evening. Without the slightest pause he shot back, "You awaken your people tomorrow. Take me out for dinner today."

Your parents want a son, not a management guru. Your spouse would rather have you with all your vulnerabilities, not a zero-defect holistic being. Your children want a father, not the father of the nation.

Haven't the two classic characters - Superman and Spider-man, taught us this? The two heroes were as vulnerable as any person - hesitant to even propose to the girls they liked. Yet, they rose to the occasion whenever the situation demanded.

I will wear my uniform and rise to the occasion in my professional world. But I will always remember that there is a time for me to remove my uniform. After all, people at home want a soul, not an evolved soul.

With my loved ones, I am what I always was.

• • •

When ego comes,
everything else goes.
When ego goes,
everything else comes.

The first major thrill after one learns cycling is to take both hands off the handlebar when the cycle is still in motion. More than the act itself, it is the fact that others notice you doing it that is important. In fact, eyes wander with longing to see if others have noticed you perform the act. Standing on the footboard of a bus or train is considered a demonstration of great courage during adolescence. The craving is not to perform the act, but to get noticed.

Everyone goes through this phase of life where the ego drives one to do anything and everything only to get noticed and recognised. It is a phase when good is good only when it gains attention; even bad is good if it can draw attention, and ironically, even good is bad if it fails to attract attention. The ego survives on gaining attention. But then, one must outgrow that phase of life.

By its very nature, ego needs feeding; and hence it is a perpetual beggar. The problem with ego is that when ego is fed, you struggle with a superiority complex, and when ego is starved you suffer from an inferiority complex. Either way, it robs you of your peace of mind.

When ego comes, everything else goes. When ego goes, everything else comes.

How many precious relationships have been lost in order to satisfy one's ego? While you should have dropped ego and saved the relationship, you ended up dropping the relationships and saving ego. Ego is never worth the losses.

How many golden opportunities have been missed while you were busy servicing your ego? Every moment is heavy, every situation is nerve-racking, every interaction is tense... an ego-filled heart is always walking on fire. Never can there be a moment of marriage between ego and ease.

A crow carrying a piece of meat found itself being chased by all the other birds. It dropped the piece of meat, and all the birds went after the meat. Now, alone in the sky, the crow remarked, "In losing that piece of meat, I gained the freedom of the skies."

There is enormous freedom in letting your ego go.

• • •

Without happiness,
there is no life.
Without dissatisfaction,
there is no growth.
Be happily dissatisfied.

She has always admired her father for his discipline. Now she is married. She expects her husband to be disciplined, which she believes is an essential virtue. In discipline, her husband never makes the grade. She is dissatisfied with him and he is frustrated with her.

"My mother has always been honest and transparent. The problem with you is that you never tell me everything about your life," the husband complains to

---

his wife. "Look at your brother's handwriting - it is a work of art, and look at yours," the mother nags the daughter. "In my earlier organisation, we never operated like this," cribs the new General Manager. "In America, we don't have these issues," cries the NRI about India.

Expectation isn't the problem; benchmarking expectation is.

She gives her father a '10 out of 10' on discipline and isn't satisfied with her husband who is tottering at 4 or 5. See, for him, 5 is his 100% score - given his nature, temperament, upbringing and conditioning, he will never make it beyond 5 on discipline. This is him and this will be him. There must be some other quality in which the husband is a perfect 10, whereas her father won't make the necessary grade. The wife may never be as transparent as the mother, but she may be very selfless in financially aiding the family. The daughter may outperform the son in singing. You believed this organisation had better growth prospects than your previous organisation, and that's why you are here. After all, India doesn't have some of the issues that the world has.

No one is inferior to others on all counts and no one is superior to the rest in all measures. We all have our pluses and we all have our minuses. No one is zero-defect. No one is all-defect. Stop focussing on isolated qualities. Start relating to the whole being.

However, there is a twist in the tale. While being dissatisfied with others makes me unhappy, being dissatisfied with myself helps me grow. When I benchmark others with my expectations, it leaves me dissatisfied with them and thus affects my happiness. When I benchmark myself with my expectations, the dissatisfaction created propels my growth and development. When I demand a '10 out of 10' from myself on excellence, integrity, purposefulness, character, competence, etc... it shows me where I stand and where I need to go. The gap becomes the scope of my transformation. When I demand a '10 out of 10' from the world, it affects the quality of my relationship with the world.

So, on all matters, rate the world on '5' and rate yourself on '10'. Not that the world is any less capable or that you are superhuman, but because... Without happiness, there is no life. So rate the world on '5'. Without dissatisfaction, there is no growth. So rate yourself on '10'. Thus you will be Happily Dissatisfied.

I am happy with the way you love me. For my part, I will find more and more ways to love you.

● ● ●

The saline waters of the ocean,
the contaminated drains,
the stinking ponds, the stagnant lakes...
...from anywhere, when water evaporates
into the above and comes down again
as rains, it is pure drinking water.

Similarly, when man connects
with the force above,
self-purification happens.
Man's thoughts, feelings and even the being
are purified when he connects with the divine.

When prayers go up, blessings come down.

Every human being has within him the potential of a new society.

W hen I look at a tree, I don't merely see a tree but a sense of history behind that tree. It could have been a seed that flew with the wind and landed on the top of a container that was later shipped from Johannesburg to Chennai.

Mother earth never pampers; so the seed had to first penetrate outside-in into the soil to root itself and then penetrate inside-out to shoot its presence. When it was a fragile plant, any animal could have grazed it, any kid could have uprooted it. Then the droughts, floods and pests. It had to withstand it all - the test of time, and the trial of circumstances - to become the majestic tree it now is. It isn't just a tree but a profound sense of history.

If it is so with a tree, what about my fellow brethren? A possible 700 million sperms dart from the man towards that one stationary egg in the woman, and only the healthiest and fastest sperm makes it. Even the very beginning of beginnings in life supports only the survival of the fittest. So, every human being is that winning sperm which proved in its own way that it was one up on the remaining 700 million of its kind. The very birth of a human being necessitates and presupposes the process of winning.

Then the growth within the womb, then the trauma of separation from the womb, the confusions, the learning, the challenges, the paradoxes, the pressures, the sacrifices, the compromises, the tears and of course, the solutions, the growing up, the joy, the potential manifested, the unlearning... each human being in his own right is a transformation from nothing to something and then into everything. A human being isn't just a human being, but a profound sense of history in his own right.

The maidservant in attempting to educate her children, by giving them the education she was deprived of, is showing in her own way that she is a sense of history. Look beyond what you see and what you hear, and you will find that you are surrounded by a humanity, with each individual carrying his own private history. In fact, you are one among them.

Every human being has within him the potential of a new society. From you begins your generation, and in turn your society. You are a profound sense of history.

● ● ●

In letting go of your hurt,
you will be letting in peace.

No single person, no single event, no single experience has the right to sit inside your head and continue to disturb the peace of your mind. Nothing... nobody... should ever be given such exalted status as to have the power over the peace of your mind. For the sake of your peace, let go of anything, let go of anybody, who continues to rattle you from within. Your mind and heart should be the seat of your peace and not the seat of someone or something that keeps disturbing you. Nothing at the cost of your peace. Everything for the sake of your peace. Learn to let go, not in the physical sense, but in an emotional sense. Free yourself of any disturbing elements. Let go whatever. Let go whoever. Put your peace above everything.

Your within can either be a basket of fragrant flowers or a vessel of acid. When you let go of the source of your hurt, you experience an inner flowering. Else, you keep destroying yourself in the same way that acid destroys the vessel that contains it.

People hurt you out of their ignorance and their immaturity. And, you allow yourself to be hurt out of your ignorance and your immaturity. The fact of the matter is that between the hater and the hated, it is always the hater who gets hurt more. While your hatred may do nothing to the other, it certainly gives you sleepless nights, causes ulcers and acidity in you, and above all, does not allow you to be at peace. So, what do you get out of living with hurt? Nobody gains and for sure, you definitely lose. Why will you live with something as meaningless as hurt?

In a physical sense, people or events that hurt you happen once. But you rewind and replay the hurt a zillion times. The more you process it, the deeper it hurts. You have given a source of disturbance a higher presence within you than your own peace.

If at all anybody is wrong, let them continue to live outside of you. Don't give them a presence within you. Let your mind and heart house only those who are a source of your peace. The rest, let them go...

In letting go of your hurt, you will let in peace. A peaceful you is a beautiful you. The good news is, you can be beautiful. The very good news is, it is in your very hands. See... even the thought of 'let go' is getting you to smile...

● ● ●

You were not born to follow.

You were born to lead.

I t seems... a mouse was in a state of constant distress because of its fear of the cat. A sage took pity on it and turned it into a cat. Now, it was afraid of the dog. So the sage turned it into a dog. Now, it was afraid of man. So the sage turned it into a man. But, the man was afraid of god. At this point the sage gave up and turned the man back to a mouse saying, "Nothing I do for you is going to be of any help because you have the heart of a mouse."

By nature, a lot of people are compulsive followers. 'Looking up to others' is a positive trait; but it becomes a weakness when it leads you into submission.

Nobody will follow a follower. When you look up to someone and also believe that they will remain so - better than you - all your life, you have grossly underestimated yourself. You have turned a blind eye to your own possibilities. As an organisation and as an individual, let anyone lead me in the first lap, the second lap, the thirteenth lap... but I've got to believe that in one of those 'n' laps, I will surge ahead and lead those who have been leading up to this point.

All of us can become better than our boss. We can all become 'The personality of life' for those who are presently 'The personality of our lives'. As many possibilities that unfold for a man we look up to, so many possibilities and more will unfold for us too. What is possible for one man is possible for all men. What one man can do, all men can do; in fact, do better.

Many people can be better than you in many aspects. This world is filled with 'one quality wonders'. Aspire to become an all-rounded personality. Take the holistic lead. Look up without submitting yourself.

You were not born to follow. You were born to lead. Remember, you were the leading sperm. Even as a sperm, you were not a follower. Live up to your inheritance.

● ● ●

Live your character at any cost; at all costs.

Anger in response to anger is more anger. Bad as a response to bad is only more bad. Wrong as a response to wrong can never be right. In life, two negatives do not make one positive. An eye for an eye and a tooth for a tooth - where will all this lead us?

We so keenly observe the enemy's traits, so much so that we eventually acquire those traits. How often in dealing with the enemy we become like the enemy!

He was a personification of honesty. However, he found himself in situations where his honesty hurt others. So he began to resort to lying, not wanting to be a source of disturbance to others. The inability to deal with his honesty was the weakness of others. Now, he has developed a weakness to counter the weakness of others. Will weakness as a response to weakness create a better world?

She has always been a plain and simple soul. Of late, she has developed the doubt that her husband is doing things that he doesn't tell her. So she has started policing him; she has been thinking of cunning ways to corner him - all traits that were never a part of her. Maybe, her husband is wrong. But thinking she is dealing with his wrongdoing, she is unaware that she is doing things that are completely out of character.

Whenever you point out someone's mistake, the immediate retort is, "What am I doing that the world isn't doing?" Never let the weaknesses of the world become a justification for your weaknesses. We don't have to become a Duryodhana to deal with Duryodhana. In fact, it is by remaining an Arjuna that you win over the Duryodhanas.

"Why do you appreciate even those who are rude to you," a teammate asked. "For the simple reason, to appreciate is my character, and to be rude is their character. I don't want other people's character to have a bearing on my character," replied the team leader.

Let us be good even to those who are not good to us. There is no justification for our stooping in character. It is not about whether others deserve our goodness or not; it's that we don't deserve anything bad in our heart or in our character.

Live your character at any cost, at all costs.

The language of life is I CAN.

I have often seen children blocking the path of an army of ants on the wall with their hands as a prank. The ants spontaneously find an alternate path and keep marching. The child now blocks even this path and the ants simply find another path and move on... The child, driven by mischief, uses his fingers to push a few ants off the wall. With resilience and spontaneity, the ants begin their climb once again. Whatever be the obstacles, however difficult the hurdles may be, the ants go on with the belief I CAN. Till they die, they try, they fight, they strive and they march on believing I CAN. They lose this sense of I CAN only to death.

I have seen bulls pull excessively overloaded carts on flyovers and overbridges. One step at a time, struggling through every inch of it, they make it. They may have been victims of man's exploitation, but all the same they never give up. Even blades of grass and the almost invisible micro-organisms keep growing against all odds with the belief I CAN. They lose this self-belief only to death.

The language of life is I CAN. The language of death is I CAN'T.

Of all the creations, man alone, supposedly the supreme of all creations, speaks the language of death. Man alone utters, believes and follows the language of death, which is I CAN'T. Research shows it is so because every human being, before he attains the age of 14, has been told by his parents, teachers, society and peer group about 1,48,000 times on an average, "YOU CAN'T". His environment has hammered into him about 1,48,000 times that "HE CAN'T".

I CAN. YOU CAN. WE CAN. Man has to rise above man. Man has to renounce the language of death and embrace the language of life. I can drop I CAN'T. I have to drop I CAN'T. I will drop I CAN'T. So what if I have been told "I CAN'T" 1,48,000 times? I have over 1,48,000 human beings in the history of humanity who have shown me that I CAN. I have every form of life to inspire me into believing I CAN. The voice of life is gradually growing louder and louder within me... this is death to the voice of death.

Let us have total faith in ourselves. Having faith in ourselves will be our way of showing faith in the wisdom that created us.

• • •

It takes what it takes,
to become
what you want to
become.

Recently, I was witness to a corporate circus. A corporate house had recruited a group of freshers who had completed their MBA in Marketing. They were asked to go to the field after two weeks of product orientation and intense training on selling skills. Within just two days of field selling, a few of them appeared highly dejected and demoralised. When asked about the cause for their disheartenment, some said, "We don't know why we are not yet able to make breakthroughs and succeed." Two days into the field and already restless about not seeing success - what a joke! I call it a corporate circus because either the two-week training by the corporate, or the two-year course on Business Management, or perhaps both, had erroneously brainwashed these fresh minds into believing in 'easy success', or put otherwise 'success is easy'. The very phrases 'easy success' and 'success is easy' sound blasphemous.

The heart really aches to see many who want to win but do not possess the willingness to prepare to win. What use is the attitude to win without the attitude to prepare to win? Even the goose capable of giving you the golden eggs has to be groomed from a gosling into an adult goose, and that takes time and effort. Imagine the idiocy of expecting eggs from a gosling that has just hatched out of an egg!

Even an uneducated person can tell you that no sportsman can exercise just a week before a game and attain the fitness level to play a match. Yet, in a country where cricket is almost a religion, the drama of conducting fitness camps just a week prior to major tournaments has been a tradition, or should I say a traditional joke for several decades? The result... you see more uncles than athletes on the cricket field.

Do you expect a trim waistline after just a week at the gym? Do you get anxious about your son's results not improving within a month of having sent him for special coaching? Do you think of a marriage counsellor just two months into marriage, frustrated that your marriage is not turning out the way you wanted it to? Do you get agitated when even after a week of trying an affectionate approach towards your rebellious teenager, she is still unrelenting?

Well, anyone who plants a seed today and expects fruits tomorrow should relocate to another planet. It isn't possible on planet earth. Here, you don't win unless you consistently and continuously back up your attitude to win with the attitude to prepare to win. Eleventh hour preparations do not work beyond the ninth standard in school. In life, preparation to win is a prerequisite to win.

Before you ask yourself or others, 'Will you win?', you'd better ask, 'Are you prepared to do what it takes to win?'

After a great piano performance in a women's club, an admirer approached the accomplished woman musician and said, "I'd give anything to play like this." The musician replied, "A lot of you promise to give anything to become what you want to, but you won't. You won't sit and practice, hour after hour, day after day, year after year."

It takes what it takes, to become what you want to become.

● ● ●

When you first cried, a new voice
that had never been heard before
was born into this world.
With your first smile, a new curve
was created, which became
a new addition to geometry.

When you were born,
you were gifted to this world
and this world was gifted to you.
Your birthday is your biggest day.

If you live well,
it will also become a big day for the world.

● ● ●

Great minds discuss ideas.
Average minds discuss events.
Small minds discuss people.

The most uncivilised activity of the civilised world is gossiping. Even the most educated and the so-called elite indulge in this uncivilised activity. Gossip is ruthless entertainment. In gossip, the tongue and the intelligence are let loose. In more ways than one, gossiping is vulgar indulgence.

In fact, people come together to form associations and clubs, and gossiping is the lifeline for their fellowship. The most dominant preoccupation of these groups is to discuss about those who are not present. Never trust a gossiper. After you leave, the one who was gossiping with you will gossip about you with others. Every gossiper will gossip about other gossipers, and this is the universal truth.

Hypocrites are those who sweet-talk on the face and bad-mouth behind your back. We shamelessly distort the images of people through gossip, without the slightest care about how much it might affect their lives. Millions of lives can be saved from the brink of suicide if only gossipers choose to be of moral support to the emotionally hurt, rather than making news out of them.

Gossip is judgement passed out of half knowledge. Every gossiper eventually drinks his own poison. He becomes highly other-people conscious. His mind is curious all the time - "What are others saying about me?" Judge not and ye shall not be judged. The contrary is also true. Judge and ye too will be judged. Gossipers live to satisfy the spectacles of others.

Curiosity and inquisitiveness are the lifelines for human evolution. When this thirst and hunger for knowledge is canalised towards realising the higher realities of life, growth happens. We make a blunder by feeding this very thirst and hunger for knowledge with gossip. Aristotle, Freud, JK and us - the quest to know is the same for everyone. If they had been gossipers, they would have been among us. If we can stop gossiping, we can be among them.

What work does a lion have among the cats? The next time the gang around you begins to gossip, just walk away. Refuse to speak or hear about those who are not present. Let our rapture not come at the cost of rupturing the hearts of other people.

Great minds discuss ideas. Average minds discuss events. Small minds discuss people.

• • •

*Good communication
will serve a relationship.
Improper communication
will sever a relationship.*

"Let me be very frank with you..."

"I am a very frank person. Whatever I want to say to people, I tell them on their face..."

"Somehow people cannot accept my frankness..."

These are lines of communication that you hear everyday. The irony is that none of these so-called frank people can accept the frankness of others when it is directed at them. When it is from them, they are just being straightforward; when it is from others, they brand it as arrogance and indifference.

Even plain facts, when expressed frankly, are difficult to accept. How then can others tolerate our frankness, which, more often than not, is just our opinion?

Truly, frankness in itself is never the problem; it is the bluntness with which our frankness is conveyed that causes the problem. Human beings are fundamentally creatures of emotions, not logic. Our frankness may have (a strong MAY HAVE) some logic in it, but the bluntness with which it is communicated emotionally ruffles other people. A wounded heart incapacitates the comprehending capabilities of the mind.

When struck by an arrow, will you sit around and analyse the raw material with which the arrow is made? When words hurt the tender hearts of people, they care too little for the meaning those words meant to convey.

It isn't just how you cook; how you serve also makes a difference. Communication achieves its objective only when all the four components are taken care of. They are - What you say, How you say, When you say, and When to stop.

Frankly speaking, good communication will serve a relationship; improper communication will sever a relationship.

● ● ●

Any work done with a selfless intent becomes god's work.

Why is there so much indifference? Don't we find it very easy to look away from people who suffer? It seems the easier route not to feel responsible or connected to the tears of the world. Let there be terrorism. Let there be hunger. Let the children of my servant-maid wear tattered clothes; so what if my driver's children don't go to school? That's their fate; I don't author their destiny. Isn't it troublesome to get involved in the pain and despair of other people? He is bearing his cross and that's his stuff. Oh, what an indifference! As long as my life is progressing on normal lines, I am able to enjoy a fine meal, a family to live for and live with, enough to promise a future, what's happening to my neighbour is of no consequence to me.

Indifference is worse than anger, more cruel than hatred, worse than revenge. At least in anger, hatred and the urge for revenge, there still exists some emotion for the other human being. Indifference reduces the other to an abstraction. Indifference numbs you of your feelings for others. In that sense, indifference is not only a sin but also a punishment.

Let us learn to feel for the last man. Let there be some sensation in our eyes when we see tears in the eyes of other people. Let us relinquish indifference. Let us begin to make a difference. We can do our part. We can play a big part. Let us not forsake those who already feel forsaken by life. Even to think we can wipe every tear from every eye may be beyond us, but as long as there are tears in the world, and as long as there is breath left in us, let our work continue.

It isn't me, but it is what I represent that defines me. Ordinary men unfold extraordinary possibilities when they identify themselves with a goal larger than themselves. Any work where the other is put ahead of myself, that very work unfolds a giant of a personality from within me. Any work done with a selfless intent becomes god's work. Barristers and schoolteachers and journalists and carpenters became revered legends only after they identified themselves with a cause larger than themselves.

The purpose of the heart is to connect to another heart. Let us learn to feel once again... all over again... When you feel for the creation, the creator feels for you.

You do not get what you desire. You only get what you deserve.

"Let all your miseries be as short-lived as your New Year resolutions," goes an Italian saying. Everybody desires to be healthy, but do they deserve it? Everyone wants to be successful, but do they deserve it?

You do not get in life what you desire; you only get what you deserve. How do you turn your desires into deservingness? When desires are backed up with Consistent Directed Self-motivated Effort (C.D.S.E.), they become deservingness.

Even effortlessness is achieved only through effort. "Genius is 1% inspiration and 99% perspiration," said Thomas Edison. A friend of mine once remarked, "If I am not as intelligent as others, I can't help it. It is god's mistake. If I am not emotionally stable, I will accept it. It is a parenting mistake. However, if I don't put in more effort than others, I will never be able to excuse myself because it'll be my mistake."

Efforts made to act on New Year resolutions never get to see February. One of the secrets of success is not to be a kick-starter, but a self-starter. Self-motivation alone is sustained motivation. The spark has to come from within.

"There is nothing so useless as doing efficiently that which should not be done at all," says Peter Drucker. Self-motivated effort without a sense of direction will be a waste of effort. What is the point in reaching the top of the ladder and then realising that the ladder is leaning against the wrong wall? Time and effort can never be managed in isolation. It is always in the context of what you want from life and where you want to reach in life. Activity without direction is change. Activity with direction is progress.

Anyone can perform an occasional act of greatness. Truly great are those who can consistently perform acts of greatness. You will not be remembered for what you do or did once in a way, but for what you do and did all the time.

'You do not get what you desire; you only get what you deserve' is His law; let it be. Let our law be - 'Through my Consistent Directed Self-motivated Effort, I will ensure that I deserve the best and only the very best in life'.

• • •

The truth you resist is the battle you fight.

When lived honestly, life heals itself. The truth you resist is the battle you fight.

You have dumped clothes inside a washing machine. The machine has performed its job. Now the clothes have to be taken out for drying. The longer you keep the clothes inside the machine, the fouler the odour will be. Don't take it out for a few days and the stench will become unbearable. So it is with our thoughts and emotions. The more and more we keep building thoughts but do not communicate, and the more and more we feel the emotions but do not express, the greater becomes the gap in the relationship. How long will you sweep things under the carpet? Eventually it will come out; and when it comes out. it will come out in unmanageable ugly proportions.

Thoughts formed but not communicated, and emotions felt but not expressed become incomplete cycles. Incomplete cycles linger alive in the subconscious. Metaphorically, the lingering incomplete cycles are like scratches formed on spectacles - anything and everything seen through the spectacles looks scratched. It is ironical that the scratches are not on the objects, but in the medium through which the objects are viewed. In all, they hamper the vision.

When you do not spontaneously communicate your thoughts and express your feelings, you begin to distort them. You tend to exaggerate or diminish the truth to placate your suppressed feelings. When you cannot face it, you tend to deny it. What you cannot accept, you pretend not to care about. As far as our incomplete cycles are concerned, time, it seems, makes a liar out of all of us.

The secret of emotional health is to tell the persons who hurt you that they hurt you, when they hurt you. Otherwise, these incomplete cycles will reappear sometime in the future and ruin even your good times.

The weight of the emotional baggage burdens the present. Something in the present will remind you of some unfinished suppression and reawaken old feelings. Those reawakened feelings will lead you to act in a way that may be completely irrelevant to the current context of your life. However, it is important to remember that old feelings resurface in order to be resolved and not to punish you. Emotional stress is purely due to thoughts not communicated and emotions not expressed. Emotional illness is a storage disease.

You are telling me, "Honestly, if I start expressing all my thoughts and feelings, I will hurt the person who matters so much to me." I am telling you, "If you don't, you will eventually hurt the relationship itself."

Let us learn to face the truth, even if it hurts. Let those who matter to us the most learn to face the truth, even if it hurts. Communicate your thoughts and feelings directly to the person who instigated it. Be prompt. Don't wait for ideal conditions. Be simple. Finish your complaint and let go. Don't exaggerate, don't nag; avoid overkill. If the person feels with you, you have succeeded. If not, understand who you are dealing with. Accept what is. Forgive and let go of your hurt. Move on... You have nothing to prove.

●●●

Even if we cannot be the solution,
let us at least be the solace.
Even if we cannot help, let us not harm.
Even if we cannot solve the problem,
let us not cause the problem.
Even if we cannot be the accelerant,
let us not be a retardant.

If you can be the pain balm
to the battered souls,
rather than being the cause of headache,
the world will come in search of you.

With compassion in words and actions,
help every man to find his solutions
and this world will belong to you.

• • •

The gates of peace open only with the keys of trust.

Irrespective of what happened to you yesterday, irrespective of what you did to the world or what the world did to you, irrespective of anything and everything, you have to wake up every morning and trust this world all over again. I know it is easier said than done, but you don't have a choice - just don't have another choice - because your peace is entwined with your trust. Without trust, there is no peace. Distrust leaves you distressed.

In the thousands of times that you may use public transport, your wallet may be picked a couple of times at the most. Even when you don't trust the world and check your wallet every few minutes, some competent, professional thief will get the better of you and pick your pocket some day... but it would have cost you a million opportunities to be peaceful otherwise. The eyes that see every co-passenger as a potential thief would have ruined your peace thousands of times, while trusting the world would have made every journey peaceful. Be wise and not otherwise.

A Nathuram Godse may get his way through, but in seeing everyone as a potential Godse you will miss a million Gandhians. Not worth it. In search of one Osama, you will have to doubt every noble heart. Not worth it.

One employee may betray your trust. Still trust the rest. A key relationship may take your goodness to be your weakness, and your trust may be exploited. Wake up another morning and start trusting all over again. I may sound naïve, but I am showing you the gates of peace, which open only with the keys of trust.

If peace is what you seek, even if you were cheated yesterday, then you don't have another choice but to wake up the next morning and trust this world all over again. Whenever I have been cheated or betrayed or hurt, I have always told myself, "Thank god that I was cheated, but I wasn't the cheat; I was betrayed, but I didn't betray; I was hurt, but I didn't hurt. Let me suffer the wrong, but never inflict the wrong."

Let us assume every morning that the world will be trustworthy from today. The world will live up to our trust a zillion times and let us down a few hundred times. The odds are tremendously in our favour. Let the heart tilt in the direction of trust.

There is only one way to peace - T.R.U.S.T.

● ● ●

You need to live
your today with tomorrow's
maturity. For him the
future awaits...

The husband manages to separately enjoy a great relationship with his wife and mother. Two arms are not enough to complete a triangle. Unless the wife and mother-in-law also enjoy a great relationship, the family triangle isn't complete. (Wondering about the father-in-law... historically, somehow he is never part of the family drama.) Every time I've listened to the wife's side of the story, the mother-in-law's side of the story and most importantly, a completely different story from the sandwiched man... one thing has been a constant - 'I am right; the other is wrong. Endorse it.'

I did a three-day program on 'Organisational Leadership' for 50 CEOs from across the country. Most questions from the participants were on the basic attitude and work ethics of their employees. I then did a one-day seminar for 300 sales professionals. In the one-to-one interactions I had with the participants, many of them expressed qualms about their organisation's approach and strategies. In both cases, one thing was constant - 'I am right; the other is wrong. Endorse it.'

For several years, I've waited outside my son's school to pick him up. Standing there, I've heard parents go on and on and on about why this approach of the school isn't acceptable and why that teacher isn't okay. I have also heard both personally and in the parent-teachers orientation programs conducted by the school authorities why parents shouldn't expect this, why this approach of parents is not acceptable, etc. Of course, the constant factor is - 'I am right; the other is wrong. You don't even have to endorse it... we know it.'

Unfortunately, life doesn't run by right and wrong. It runs on maturity. In any situation, it's not about who is right and who is wrong; the need is always for a mature mind that can accept differences as a way of life and manage the situation.

If your mother-in-law complains about everything... that's her nature. If your daughter-in-law criticises you for everything... that's her limitation. If your wife and mother are at loggerheads, now you have a situation to manage... you have decisions to make and standpoints to take. Cribbing, condemning and crying changes nothing. Problems in a family exist not because it involves people, but because it involves immature people. Even if one mature mind is present, the situation can be managed and harmony built. As an employee, either find ways to excel with the ways of this organisation or find an organisation that works your way.

So often, by just letting people have their way, your way becomes clear. The truth is simple and straight. If there is a problem, there is an immature mind involved in it. If there is a solution, there is a mature mind dealing with it. In any situation, there is a level from which right and wrong is perceptible. There is another level just above it, from which only solutions are visible. Just lift yourself a little above the common plane; there is a different reality awaiting you.

It is not enough to look at your yesterday with today's maturity. You need to live your today with tomorrow's maturity. For him the future awaits...

● ● ●

Guru is the one who liberates you.

It is a relationship of deep love,
reverence, surrender, and faith.

A guru creates, transforms and
gives a new birth to a seeker.

Guru is one with inexplicable gravitation.
There is a constant pull... an invitation.
There is something truly magnetic.

Guru is a presence,
a presence that transforms
the very chemistry of your being.

• • •

Every good human being has the moral responsibility to be rich.

I f we find ourselves living in a tarnished society, a lot of good human beings are responsible for it. The problem with most good human beings is that they are very contented and satisfied with their lives. They are so sufficient unto themselves that they have no urge to be rich... they feel no emotional compulsion for financial abundance.

Let's say, there's a hundred rupee note lying on the road. A good human being will walk past it saying to himself, "This is not my money. So I will not touch it." What he left behind, a rascal picks up. Even if he had no desire to own it, if only the good human being had picked up that hundred rupee note, he could have used it to feed the poor. By ignoring it, he left the money for a rascal who is bound to use it for destructive purpose.

The amount of official currency in circulation in any country is constant. Now, the money can either be with a good human being or with a scoundrel. The unwillingness of good human beings to amass wealth because of a sense of contentment has made available voluminous amounts of money to evil forces. Beyond a point, prosperity creates a surplus for anyone. But the difference is, surplus in the hands of a good human being will be used to create a better world; the same surplus in the hands of an unethical, insensitive, evil-minded person will be used to destroy the world. A good human being will use the surplus to build schools, improve the environment, fund education, feed the poor, extend medical help. The unscrupulous element will drop bombs, train suicide squads, create religious disharmony, kill innocent people.

Think of surplus in the hands of Mother Teresa. Also think of surplus resources in the hands of Osama.

My call is to all good human beings to put their hands up and be counted in building a fraternity of prosperous people... good people who will not sell their conscience. Let's not leave behind a hundred rupee note for evil forces. Let us weaken them. Let us take financial control. Let us build a financial surplus. You may not need so much. So what? Let us use it to build a better world.

Let me be categorical. Every good human being has the moral responsibility to be rich.

• • •

If we remove the teachings of our teachers from us, nothing of us will remain.

amakant Acharekar was not a better cricketer than Sachin Tendulkar. Yet, it was his coaching that showed Sachin to Sachin, and in turn showed him to the world. O.M.Nambiar was no match for P.T.Usha, but it was he who gave India one of the greatest athletes. The glory of Dronacharya was to have developed Arjuna to the point where Arjuna was able to win the battle with his own teacher.

We need someone outside of us to guide us. They are the mirrors that reflect us to ourselves, that show us the strengths with which we can fight our weaknesses. We need coaches to sharpen our skills. We need teachers to expand our knowledge. We need gurus to realise our spiritual self.

Your nursery school teacher may not have made it as big as you in life, but your life was built on the foundation of knowledge she gave you. Let us not compare ourselves with our guiding light. If you remove the sun from the rays, nothing will remain. If you remove the mud from the pot, nothing will remain. If you remove the cause from the effect, nothing remains. If we remove the teachings of our teachers from us, nothing of us will remain.

The maths teacher wrote '1000' on the board and asked the student who was constantly disturbing the class, "How much is this?" Confident, yet embarrassed by the simplicity of the question, the boy replied, "One thousand." Now the teacher added a zero to the right and pointing at '10000' asked, "How much is this?" "Ten thousand," came the prompt reply. Now the teacher added another zero, but this time to the left of '1' and pointing at '010000' again enquired, "How much now?" "The same... ten thousand," the boy replied. The teacher smiled, winked and then said, "When an insignificant number follows a significant number, it gains value. When the same insignificant number tries to go ahead of the significant number, then it has no value. So is the relationship between a teacher and a student. When a student follows the teacher, he gains value. The other way round... well, I don't want to state the obvious."

The greatness of a coach is to show the player how capable he is. The greatness of a player is to live up to the capability he has been shown.

● ● ●

Change when monitored and sustained long enough becomes a culture.

How tiring it is to be caught up in the vicious cycle of changing and losing that change, only to change again and lose it...

Sometime back, a law was enacted in Chennai prohibiting smoking in public places. Who cares? You still find people smoking everywhere. Singapore too had enacted a law a couple of decades ago against littering. Everyone obeys it! Why? What is the difference? Adherence to the law is not monitored in Chennai, whereas it is monitored in Singapore.

Change when monitored and sustained long enough becomes a culture. The challenge isn't change, but the transformation of that change into a culture.

The law against smoking in public places has not been supported by competent systems or personnel to monitor its enforcement. So the law in effect remains just a law in the book and not in practice. However, littering was strictly monitored in Singapore; hence the change was sustained and today it has become the culture of Singapore.

A good training program, a good book, a spiritual discourse or an external stimulant like the New Year certainly motivates most of us to change. The only drawback with these changes is that they die an instant death if they are not monitored. To change and then to lose that change makes one psychologically impotent - be it the government, an institution, or an organisation.

What separates the legends from the rest of the world? Whenever legends embrace change, they monitor and sustain the change till it becomes their culture. On the contrary, the rest of the world embraces temporary changes only to lose them, for want of monitoring them. Then they wait once again for another occasion like the New Year or another motivational training program and again attempt the same changes that they have already attempted and failed.

If change is monitored and sustained till it becomes your culture, then your life will be an upward spiral. Else it will be a vicious cycle.

Why at all begin if you are going to end at the same place?

● ● ●

Looking up to others is a positive trait, but it becomes a weakness when it leads you into submission. Look up without submitting yourself. You can become better than your boss. What is possible for one man is possible for all men. What one man can do, all men can do; in fact, do better. You were not born to follow. Remember, you were the leading sperm. Even as a sperm, you were not a follower. You were born to lead. Live up to your inheritance.

Have you read our Complete Growth Magazine

infinithoughts

infinithoughts has gone on to transform millions of lives and is being experienced by lakhs of readers every month in more than 35 countries!

infinithoughts is the answer to all questions on life. It is a manual on life. It is a guide to successful and peaceful living. It will motivate you, urge you to become better – to become the best that you can be.

To subscribe please log on to **www.infinitheism.com**